Stephen Ed. Grove

Souvenir and Guide Book of Harper's Ferry, Antietam and South Mountain

Stephen Ed. Grove

Souvenir and Guide Book of Harper's Ferry, Antietam and South Mountain

ISBN/EAN: 9783337289072

Printed in Europe, USA, Canada, Australia, Japan

Cover: Foto ©Lupo / pixelio.de

More available books at **www.hansebooks.com**

SOUVENIR...

AND GUIDE BOOK

———OF———

HARPER'S FERRY, ANTIETAM AND SOUTH MOUNTAIN

....BATTLEFIELDS.

❧ ❧ ❧

——BY——

S. ED. GROVE,
HARPER'S FERRY,
...W. VA...

❧ ❧ ❧

PRESS OF
THOMPSON BROTHERS,
MARTINSBURG,
W. VA.
1898

PREFACE.

I have no doubt disappointed very many of my friends and I have scarcely half improved the opportunity that laid before me in the compilation of this little SOUVENIR AND GUIDE BOOK, yet I feel that I have met a want and linked together two events in history that are peculiarly fitted to be thus associated.

What Brown's Raid failed to accomplish on Oct. 16th, 1859, was made possible three years later by the battles of Antietam and South Mountain, fought nearly upon the same spot. What the poor wool-dealer and his followers failed to do unlawfully, was done as a measure of war by the U. S. Government upon the issue of these battles.

I have reference to the Emancipation Proclamation, issued Jan. 1st, 1863.

The provisions of the Chatham Constitution, over which Brown would liked to have remodeled the government (given elsewhere) are virtually the same as the present Constitution, slavery being omitted. And the crowning results of the war, no doubt, surpasses the most roseate dreams of the raiders.

I have no war prejudices and was but a little boy in kilts at the time, and remember but its pomp. I view the results through honest spectacles. I do not assume the sole authorship of the little book, either ; a number of friends contributed to its success. Principally is Dr. Thos. Fatherstonhaugh, Washington, D. C., who contributed photos of all the raiders and their legal prosecutors and counsel, without which the book would have been divested of much of its interest.

Others contributed willingly and abundantly in various directions, for all which I herewith extend my most heartfelt gratitude.

HARPER'S FERRY, WEST VIRGINIA.

❧ Harper's Ferry. ❧

Whether I shall call this book a souvenir of the gorgeous scenery that breaks upon the eye, or the great natural gateway of the Potomac and Shenandoah rivers, as they embrace and flow to the sea, or the outlet of the great western traffic that seeks the seaboard for foreign distribution over the first, and possibly the greatest, trunk-line in existence, or should name it the U. S. Armory, established long years ago, by the illustrious citizen "who was first in war, first in peace and first in the hearts of his countrymen," or by the more recent but no less significant event, John Brown's raid—each and all would point with unerring finger to Harper's Ferry.

People of other lands who are found ignorant of important American cities, know of Harper's Ferry, and, thus, its fame is world-wide.

Thomas Jefferson has said, in his notes on Virginia, "This scene is worth a voyage across the Atlantic," and a chorus of amens have followed in its confirmation. The mountains, consisting of Maryland, Loudoun and Bolivar heights, are known as Harper's Ferry, and stand 1700 feet above sea level, and 600 feet above the surrounding country, with an abiding river air, which makes it an admirable summer resort.

It is beautiful in all its aspects. The rays of the morning sun bursting upon its dew-dipped mountains and valleys; its evening rays falling upon and lighting, with gold, its mountain peaks and cloud-flecked heavens, and under the silver-sheen of the more mellow moonlight, the scene is placed beyond the pen to describe.

The Fall brings the varied colors of the autumnal foliage which possesses a richer lustre under the more slantern and golden sun, and which, with the silvery surface and music of the rivers, make enchantment complete.

Bolivar Heights is an inspiration.

A lofty wooded summit, extending from the Potomac to Shenandoah river and facing the great mountain gap at Harper's Ferry, it commands a full sweep of the Blue Ridge from Maryland and Pennsylvania on the left to Luray, Va., on the right. Westward, across the Shenandoah Valley, is seen the North Mountains, stretching from Pennsylvania, ninety miles to the West of Woodstock, Va. Between these two great mountain chains, to the northward, are the superb views of the Potomac, and beyond lie the battle-scarred foothills of the Blue Ridge, extending eastward from Antietam. The cultivated field and improved farms that lie in the valley and upon the tablelands diversify the landscape with good effect. Besides, it contains ruined ramparts of the late civil war, and marks the surrender and death of Col. Miles.

Camp Hill lies on a subdued bluff, east of Bolivar Heights, and Harper's Ferry, proper, at its feet, upon a tongue of land that gradually slopes into the river. History and world-wide science keep perpetual school here.

The canal boat threads its slow and weary way beneath the shadow of the winding mountains of the Maryland side, while opposite the fast express train hugs the foot of the heights and shoots in and out upon its serpentine track, like a darting sparrow.

The clouds of smoke belching from engines struggling with heavy freight trains through the tunnel and up an ascending grade, along with the dam of the pulp mill, where fishing and rowing are indulged in and sometimes a steam yacht plys, add variety and interest still further to the scenery of the place.

ST. PETER'S CATHOLIC CHURCH.

Written by a Visitor.

"On a cliff of a hill at the Ferry
   At a point where two rivers meet,
Stands St. Peter's, so stately and airy,
   The town nestling down at its feet.

Before it, in rapturous beauty,
   Rise mountains with peaks in the sky,
While behind it, as soldier on duty,
   Old "Jefferson's Rock" greets the eye.

Was there ever a scene more uplifting?
   Was there ever a vision more fair
Than this fane in an era of drifting,
   Encircled by mounts in the air."

ST. PETER'S CATHOLIC CHURCH.

Visitors' Opinion of Harper's Ferry.

Special Cor. Columbian.

WASHINGTON, D. C., July 27, 1897.

Having a day's holiday, I utilized it by paying a visit to Harper's Ferry, which I had never seen in daylight. The geography I studied, in my youth, credited Thomas Jefferson with stating that this locality is one of the most stupendous scenes in nature, and I have always had a desire to gaze upon it. There are mighty changes, through man's handiwork, since Jefferson's time, but these, if anything, add to the majesty or rather to the diversified picturesqueness of the spectacle. By the B. &. O. fast trains the trip is delightful as well as rapid. There is a constant change of aspect, from the car window. The suburbs of Washington have been splendidly improved and the charming scenery of villa sites and new hamlets extend for miles. An hour's run brings us to the upper Potomac and the canal along its banks, which winds from Georgetown to Cumberland. Slow as is the boat transit, much bulky merchandise, chiefly coal, is transported. I suppose that swift trains do not annoy the boatmn, because, like the traditional skinned eel, "they be used to it."

* * *

THE GRAND, BEAUTIFUL AND HISTORIC.

At a place called Buchanan, the B. & O. concentrates many locomotives and cars along a wilderness of tracks, and one can see, at a glance, how tremendous is the equipment of the system. Here, too, the mountains rise gigantically. Penetrating a tunnel, the splendid and sublimely beautiful location of Harper's Ferry bursts upon the vision. Here the Potomac cleaves through the Blue Ridge, eager to embrace the Shenandoah, which rushes to the contact from its West Virginia barricade. The town of Harper's Ferry is situated on a tongue of land formed by the two rivers. It is a rocky height, with the towering cliffs of Maryland and Virginia on either side. Across the rivers are numerous spans of iron bridges for railway passage and vehicles of the farmer. Here the B. & O. branches toward the Virginia Valley where Lee and Jackson sleep in death. Just at the apex of the bridges is a small granite monument indicating the site of John Brown's fort.

* * *

ON THE HEIGHTS.

I climbed the steep acclivities of High street and reached the top of Bolivar Heights, where there is a hotel. Along the street were many pretty dwellings and excellent gardens. Emerging from the avenue I strolled to a vacant lot and sat upon a stone to leisurely observe the panorama. Far below, the Potomac surged over innumerable ledges, foaming through rocks and fretting against a small island. The mighty mountain rampart of Maryland rose beyond, while at its base the canal threaded a sluggish way. Just above, a dam impounded the waters for a pulp mill. On the near side, the steel tracks of the B. & O. were visible, and many trains thundered by shriekingly. When I had seen enough, for the time, I descended the Heights by another route, and near the base, but still on an elevated plateau, overlooking the mingling of the waters. I came to the residence of the Catholic pastor, Father Kelly. To reach his door, I had to cross a bridge. Very regretfully I heard that he was absent. Just above the rectory is a venerable, dilapidated and deserted Episcopal church, where Catholics were holding a festival. On a line with the priest's house, a handsome granite church is in course of erection for our brethren. It is dedicated to St. Peter, and pious folks must climb steep steps, hewn in the rock, to reach it. Luckily they are accustomed to such pedestrianism. The Catholic congregation is the largest numerically and I heard that it was about to be increased by converts who dwell on the Loudoun Heights of Virginia.

Souvenir of the Summer of 1896.

A MOUNTAIN SPIRIT ? IN CLOUD LAND.

On the mountain side, alone with sweet memory of happy hours that are past, the declining day brings the witching hour of twilight. Through lace-like clouds, spun by unseen angel hands, we see this spirit carrying a "message" of love to loved ones that are absent.

CHIMNEY ROCK.

A man of gentle birth with simple taste and habit, leaves his ancestral home in rock-ribbed New England and follows the homing birds of song to the sunny land of the South, and there finds a mate. The "honey-moon" lasts the life of a beautiful loving woman—then the angel of death closes the portal of happiness to a stricken heart—an ever present tragedy ! * * *

The scene changes : more than twenty-five years have passed, leaving the marks of time—but the *heart* of the man remains young and feels the sensation of desire, hope, anticipation, inspiration and gratitude. Since those days of sorrow, solitude

alone has claimed his attention and primeval forest has been his *Alma Mater.* Nature has been his teacher. Rustic roads o'ershadowed by leaf and tree, with open vistas of peaceful valley, cloud-tipped mountains, garland homes and winding paths to springs of limpid waters, become familiar, and comradeship of congenial spirits, and kind and loving attentions marked these highways of human life, as milestones on the way to the home of the blest !

This beautiful Spirit of refinement and grace, around which hovers the presence of the Dove of Peace—long ago the bright harbinger of promise, comes like an inspiration into this old man's life ; and he lives again ! and the fire of youth thrills his heart with new impulse, and the tragedy of his young days fade away ; while he listens to the voice of this sentient being, so exquisite, sympathetic and beautiful is its harmony.

On the mountain top !

The winding paths by boulder rock o'ergrown with moss and fern, where once the raging water ran, this Spirit, more mortal than divine and more *spirituelle* than mortal, passed in and out before our eyes, a very *San Buouventura* and beneficence !

From an open vista a world of beauty and surpassing wonder lies at our feet ! Mountains rear their hoary heads, flowing rivers wind their silver sheen through "Pleasant Valleys," and modest homes dot the landscape o'er—a picture of rural contentment and peace. A great thought thrills again an expectant heart. Some day ? on the breast of dear loving Mother-Nature, will lie the precious body of those we love, while the spirit takes its flight beyond the clouds we see, beyond the ether-blue, beyond the fading and fadeless stars of hope to the realms of eternal rest !

Something tells us we shall always know those we have met and loved in this life.

But for the passing moment I still can say :

" Oh stay, thou art so fair."

J. W. FARRAR.

CLIPPED FROM HARPER'S FERRY SENTINEL.

There is no finer scenery this side of the "Rockies." It is of surpassing beauty and grandeur—mountain upon mountain range greet one from every point of the compass. The valleys and table-lands are covered with cultivation, and picturesque homes of a kindly and hospitable people. Winding roads take one through primeval forests where every form of flora is pleasing to the eye of the artist, a charm to the sense of the refined; all of which impress the lover of Nature with the wonders of her kingdom. The far-famed Shenandoah Valley is in sight from every hill-top, mountain range and high table-land; cool breezes, wafted from pine forests and healing balsam that fill the air with aromatic perfume. It is here more than anywhere that Nature meets you with a welcome that is as generous as it is kind, and where people are hospitable without effusiveness and charitable without cant.

Maryland, Loudoun and Bolivar Heights stand as great sentinels to guard the open door of the historic Potomac and beautiful Shenandoah as they break away from their embrace and flow onward toward the mighty ocean.

Upon these heights will stand, some day in the near future, modern hotels, whose sumptuous appointments of flashing light, sparkling fountains and intoxicating music, will attract the rich, the educated, the artist, the poet, the *literati*, and the man of affairs. These in turn will induce others of like taste and environment to come here and build cottages, and out of those there will be found brave and energetic spirits who take counsel of their judgment and will turn this vast waste of water to some better use than carrying water to market in a sieve. All sentiment aside, There is no reason why Maryland and Virginia should not be as populous as France, Belgium or Germany. We certainly are as intelligent and far more enterprising. In those foreign countries rivers like the Potomac and Shenandoah would have hundreds of mills giving employment to many populous cities. The music of whirling spindles, throbbing looms and vibrating machinery ought now to be heard at Harper's Ferry, in place of the *Dolce*

GRAVES OF SOME OF BROWN'S FOLLOWERS, ON THE SHENANDOAH RIVER AT HARPER'S FERRY.

far niente of the well-to-do and the *siesta* of the indifferent.

These mid-Southern States could get all the supplies that enter the home and are used upon the farm, and in the factory, right at their very doors, by investing their capital in a great manufacturing plant at Harper's Ferry.

JOHN BROWN'S FORT.

Authority is given for the statement that army officers are ready to make investments here just as soon as proper inducements are guaranteed as to reasonableness of price. This is a subject that should receive the attention of all those who are interested in the welfare of the two towns of Harper's Ferry and Bolivar.

It is when prominent men of means are induced to invest and settle here that one may expect a rise in values, and it is through their presence and interest that others are tempted to come. It is population that makes land valuable.

In this high altitude the dawn and twilight, with great mountain ranges for a back-ground, suggest to the artist an inspiration for his brush, the poet a theme for his fancy, the lover an opportunity, while the care-worn and weary find here the rest and solace they so greatly desire. Here will be found pure water, exhilarating air and the silence of nature that follows you through the wakeful hours of the day, when twilight comes with sunset glories so transcendently beautiful that one's thoughts are insensibly carried beyond the fadeless stars to the mysteries of the unknown! The dawn; well, yes, one does have to get up early to witness the changing hue of sky and mountain top; but one is repaid, for it is then that the song birds fly away from their night-nests to meet their mates, singing as they go, making the air resonant with songs of their love-making. As the sun's rays penetrate vale and glen they are transformed into bowers where Nature makes her toilet and dew-drops hang pendant like diamonds, pearls and sapphires! This whole country is historic with legends of battle, romance, folk-lore, song and story. All this wealth of dense forest, running streams of water from cool mountain springs, towering heights, cloud-caped and luminous with golden sun and glow of softer sheen from silver moon, is at the very doors of the capital of a mighty empire! whose destiny will yet control the mind, fashion, ethics, invention and philosophy of the world!

   ✻   ✻   ✻

SCOTTISH CASTLE, ON BOLIVAR HEIGHTS,
SUMMER RESIDENCE OF JUDGE VANE.

BROWN AND HIS FOLLOWERS.

John Brown's Raid.

The most interesting historical feature of Harper's Ferry is John Brown's Raid. Its fame is as intimately and inseparably linked with the town as that of its beautiful scenery.

Brown and his men (Kansas Regulars, in part,) came here from bloody Kansas, where they had been operating to free the slaves, by making that state free in the sisterhood of states.

The President had put a reward of $3000 upon the old man, besides he possessed a number of *aliases*, by which he eluded the law in his work of freedom, and the soubriquet of "Hero of Ossawatomie," he won in a battle by that name. The following is a description of the famous engagement : "With his force of thirty men, Brown fought the enemy from ambush. One of Brown's party was killed and three wounded. The enemy lost thirty-one killed, with from fifty to sixty wounded. The Missourians fled, after setting fire to the houses of Brown's sons. After the battle, the old man and his companions stood upon a hill overlooking Ossawatomie, and watched the destruction of their homes by fire. Brown stood with folded arms, looking at the smoke of the burning buildings as they were fired, one by one, by the Missourians, and turning to his son, Jason, he said :

"God sees it ! There will be no more real peace in this country until the slavery question is settled. I have no feelings of revenge towards the people of the South. I have but a little while to live, and but one death to die. I will die fighting slavery.'"

This result verifies the truth of John Brown's assertion, that one man fighting for freedom was worth five paid soldiers on the other side. The Missourians had 400 or more men.

A pro-slavery preacher, named Martin White, had, on the previous day, shot and killed his son, Fred. K. Brown, on the public highway, and after the boy was lying dead in the roadway fired a pistol shot into the open mouth of the body. White was afterwards elected to the Territorial Legislature, and gave a laughable account of the killing in the Assembly. At the close of the session, White's corpse was found cold and stiff on the prairie, on the road leading to his home.

The following is a characteristic speech made by John Brown, from a store box on the main street of Lawrence, Kansas, upon the expected attack of 1000 Missourians upon the town :

"Gentlemen, it is said that there are twenty-five hundred Missourians down at Franklin, and that they will be here in two hours. You can see for yourselves the smoke they are making by setting fire to the houses in that town. Now is probably the last opportunity you will have of seeing a fight ; so that you had better do your best. If they should come up and attack us, don't yell and make a great noise, but remain perfectly silent and still. Wait till they get within twenty-five yards of you ; get a good object ; be sure you see the hind sight of your gun, then fire. A great deal of powder and lead and very precious time is wasted by shooting too high. You had better aim at their legs than at their heads. In either case be sure of the hind sights of your guns. It is from this reason that I myself have so many times escaped ; for, if all the bullets which have ever been aimed at me had hit me, I would have been as full of holes as a riddle."

Brown's share in this bloody campaign was a burnt home, dead son, another almost a raving maniac by ill-treatment when a prisoner, a third son and son-in-law wounded from gun shots from Missourians, and himself reduced in health. This was in the latter part of 1856, and in the Summer of 1859, two years and a half later, he and his confeds, as I remarked previously, turned up at Harper's Ferry. The following is a terse and graphic description given in the "Annals of Harper's Ferry," written by one of its citizens, Joseph Berry, who was an eye witness of the event from start to finish, i. e., close of the war :

During the summer of 1859, a party of strange men made their appearance at Sandy Hook, a small village in Washington county, Maryland, in the immediate vicinity of Harper's Ferry. With them, was an old man of venerable appearance and austere demeanor who called himself Smith. They represented themselves as prospecting for minerals and they took frequent and long rambles, with this ostensible purpose, over the various peaks of the Blue Ridge Mountains. They, at first, boarded at the house of Mr. Ormand Butler, where their conduct was unexceptionable. They paid in gold for whatever they purchased, and, as their manners were courteous to all, they were, on the whole, very popular. After a few weeks' stay at Sandy Hook they removed to what is called "The Kennedy Farm," about five miles from Harper's Ferry, on the Maryland side of the Po-

tomac, where they established their headquarters. While at
"The Kennedy Farm," Smith and his party, of whom three
were his sons, made themselves very agreeable to their
neighbors and they were as popular there as they had been at
Sandy Hook. The father was regarded as a man of stern moral-
ity, devoted to church exercises, and the sons, with the others of
the party, as good-natured, amiable young men. Thus, things
continued, 'til the night of Sunday, October 16th, 1859. On
that night, a little after 10 o'clock, Mr. William Williams, one
of the watchmen on the railroad bridge, was surprised to find
himself taken prisoner by an armed party, consisting of about
twenty men, who suddenly made their appearance from the
Maryland side of the river. Most of the party then proceeded
to the Armory enclosure, taking with them their prisoner
and leaving two men to guard the bridge. They next captured
Daniel Whelan, one of the watchmen at the Armory, who was
posted at the front gate, and they took possession of that estab-
tablishment. The party then divided themselves into two
bodies, one remaining in the Armory and the other proceeding
to the Rifle Factory, half a mile up the Shenandoah, where they
captured Mr. Samuel Williams, (father of William Williams,
before mentioned,) an old and highly respected man, who was in
charge of the buildings as night watchman. He was conducted
to the Armory, where the other prisoners were confined, and a
detachment of the strangers was left to supply his place.
About 12 o'clock Mr. Patrick Higgins, of Sandy Hook, arrived
on the bridge, for the purpose of relieving Mr. William Williams. They were both in the employ of the Baltimore and
Ohio Railroad Company as watchmen and each was to serve
twelve hours of the twenty-four, on duty. Higgins found all in
darkness and, suspecting that something had gone wrong with
Williams, he called loudly for him. To his astonishment he
was ordered to halt and two men presented guns at his breast, at
the same time telling him he was their prisoner. One of them
undertook to conduct him to the Armory but, on arriving near
the Virginia end of the bridge, the hot-blooded Celt struck his
captor a stunning blow with his fist and, before the stranger
could recover from its effects, Higgins had succeeded in escaping
to Fouke's Hotel, where he eluded all pursuit. Several shots were
fired after him without effect, and he attributes his safety to the
fact that his pursuers stumbled in the darkness, over some cross-
pieces in the bridge.

About this time a party of the invaders went to the

houses of Messrs. Washington and Allstadt, living a few miles from Harper's Ferry and took them and some of their slaves prisoners, conducting them to the general rendezvous for their captives—the Armory enclosure. From the house of the former, they took some relics of the great Washington and the Revolution, which the proprietor, of course, very highly prized. Among them was a sword, said to be the same that was sent to General Washington by Frederick The Great, King of Prussia—a present, (as a legend inscribed on it said,) from the oldest General of the time to the best. All through the night, great excitement existed among such of the citizens as became cognizant of these facts. About 1 o'clock the Eastward bound Express Train, on the Baltimore and Ohio Railroad, arrived, in charge of Conductor Phelps. The train was detained by order of the leader of the band and the telegraph wires were cut. The object of these orders was, of course, to prevent news of these proceedings being spread. The train was, however, allowed to proceed after a considerable delay. While the train was at Harper's Ferry, great excitement naturally existed among the passengers, who could not understand these movements. Several shots were exchanged between the attacking force and a Mr. Throckmorton, clerk at Fouke's Hotel, and some other parties unknown, but no person was injured. Some time, in the course of the night, Hepwood Shepherd, a colored porter at the Railroad office, walked to the bridge, impelled, no doubt, by curiosity to understand the enigma. He was ordered to halt by the guards at the bridge, and, being seized with a panic and running back, was shot through the body. He succeeded in reaching the Railroad office where he died next day at 3 o'clock, in great agony.

A little before daylight, some early risers were surprised to find themselves taken prisoners, as soon as they appeared on the streets, and marched to the Armory. Among them, was James

THOS. ALLSTADT.
BROWN'S SURVIVING HOSTAGE.

Darrel, aged about sixty years, the bell-ringer at the Armory, whose duties, of course, compelled him to be first of the Armory hands at his post. It being yet dark, he carried a lantern. When near the gate, he was halted by an armed negro, one of the invading party, and Darrell, not dreaming of what was transpiring, and mistaking his assailant for one of Mr. Fouke's negroes on a "bender," struck him with his lantern and consigned his "black soul" to a climate of much higher temperature than that of Virginia. The negro presented a Sharp's Rifle at Darrell and, no doubt, the situation of Bell-Ringer at Harper's Ferry Armory would very soon have been vacant, had not a white man of the party who appeared to relish very highly the joke of the mistake, caught the gun and prevented the negro from carrying out his intention. Another white man of the party, however, came up and struck Darrell on the side with the butt end of his gun, injuring him severely. Darrell was then dragged before "the Captain," who, pitying his age and his bodily sufferings, dismissed him on a sort of parole. Mr. Walter Kemp, an aged, infirm man, bartender at Mr. Fouke's Hotel, was, about this time, taken a prisoner and consigned to limbo with the others.

It was now day-light and the Armorers proceeded, singly and in parties of two and three, from their various houses, to work at the shops. They were gobbled up in detail and marched to prison, lost in astonishment at these strange proceedings and many, perhaps, doubting if they were not yet asleep and dreaming. Several of the officers of the Armory were captured, but the Superintendent not being in town at the time, the invaders missed what, no doubt, would have been, to them, a much desired prize. About this time, Mr. George W. Cutshaw, an old and estimable citizen, proceeded from his house, on High street, towards the bridge in company with a lady who was on her way to Washington City and whom Mr. Cutshaw was escorting across the bridge, to the place where the Canal Packet Boat on which the lady intended to travel, was moored. He passed along unmolested until he disposed of the lady, but on his return, he encountered on the bridge several armed apparitions, and was, therefore, immediately marched off to the Armory, among the other prisoners.

A little before 7 o'clock, Mr. Alexander Kelly approached the corner of High and Shenandoah streets, armed with a shotgun, for the purpose of having a shot at the invaders. No sooner did he turn the corner, than two shots were fired at him, and a bullet was sent through his hat. Immediately afterwards, Mr. Thomas Boerly approached the corner, with the same purpose. He was a man of Herculean strength and great personal courage. He discharged his gun at some of the enemy who were standing at the Arsenal gate, when a shot was fired at him, by one of the party who was crouching behind the fence. The bullet penetrated his groin, inflicting a ghastly wound of which he died in a few hours.

It was, now, breakfast time and "the Captain" sent an order to Fouke's Hotel, for refreshments for his men. It is not known what the state of his exchequer was, but he did not pay for the breakfasts in any usual species of currency. He released Walter—familiarly called Watty—Kemp, the bar-tender and he announced this as the equivalent he was willing to pay. It is to be feared that Mr. Fouke did not duly appreciate the advantages he gained by this profitable bargain and it may be that "Uncle Watty," himself, did not feel much flattered at the estimate put on him, in the terms of the ransom, and his being deemed an equivalent for twenty breakfasts. Be this as it may, the bargain was struck and the grub provided. "The Captain" invited his prisoners to partake of the refreshments, but only a few accepted the invitation, for fear of the food being drugged.

Up to this time no person in the town, except the prisoners, could tell who the party were. To them, as was afterwards ascertained, the party confessed their purpose of liberating the slaves of Virginia, and freedom was offered to any captive who would furnish a negro man as a recruit for "the army of the Lord." As, however, there was little or no communication allowed between the prisoners and their friends outside, the people generally were yet ignorant of the names, number and purposes of the strangers and, as may well be imagined, Madam Rumor had plenty of employment for her hundred tongues. Soon, however, they were recognized by some as the mineral explorers and suspicion at once rested on a man named John E. Cook, who had been sojourning at Harper's Ferry for some years, in the various capacities of school-master, book-peddler and lock-keeper on the Chesapeake and Ohio Canal, and who had married into a respectable family at that place. He had been seen associating with the Smith party and as he had often been heard to boast of his exploits in "the Kansas war," on the Free-Soil side, it was instinctively guessed that he and the Smiths were connected in some project for freeing the slaves, and this opinion was confirmed by the fact of there being armed negroes in the party.

Shortly after, a new light broke on the people and it was ascertained that "The Captain" was no other than the redoubtable John Brown, of Kansas notoriety, who had earned the title of "Ossawattomie Brown," from his exploits in the portion of Kansas, along the banks of the Ossawattomie river. The information came from one of the prisoners (Mr. Mills) who was allowed to communicate with his family.

At a regular hour for commencing work in the morning, Mr. Daniel J. Young, Master Machinist at the Rifle Factory, approached the gate to those shops, expecting to find Mr. Samuel Williams at his post, and little anticipating to find the place in possession of an enemy. He was met at the gate by a fierce looking man, fully armed, who refused him admittance, claiming that he and his companions (four or five of whom appeared at the watch-house door, on hearing the conversation,) had gotten possession by authority from the Great Jehovah. Mr. Young, being naturally astonished at hearing this, asked what the object of the strangers was, and was informed that they had come to give freedom to the slaves of Virginia ; that the friends of liberty had tried every constitutional and peaceable means to accomplish this end and had signally failed, but that now, the great evil of slavery must be eradicated at any risk, and that there were means enough ready to accomplish this purpose. Mr. Young remarked, in reply : "If you derive your authority from the Almighty, I must yield, as *I* derive my right to enter from an earthly power—the United States Government. I warn you, however, that before this day's sun sets, you and your companions will be corpses. Mr. Young then went back to stop the mechanics and laborers who were on their way to go to work, and warn them of their danger. It appeared to be no part of the policy of the strangers to keep prisoners at the Rifle Works, as no attempt was made to arrest Mr. Young.

About 9 o'clock the people had recovered from their amazement and furnished themselves with arms. This was no easy matter, as the Arsenal and nearly all the store-houses were in possession of the enemy. It was recollected, however, that some time before, a lot of guns had been removed from the place where they were usually stored, in order to protect them from the river, which at the time had over-flowed its banks and encroached on the Armory. Enough was procured from this lot to equip a few small companies of citizens and a desultory engagement commenced around the Armory building and the adjacent streets, which continued all day. A company under Captain

Medler, crossed the Shenandoah on the bridge and took post on the Loudoun side of the river, opposite the Rifle Factory. Another company, under Captain Roderick, took position on the Baltimore and Ohio Railroad, North-west of the Armory, and a third body, under Captain Moore, crossed the Potomac about a mile above Harper's Ferry, and marched down on the Maryland side to take possession of the railroad bridge. Brown's party were thus hemmed in and all the citizens who were not enrolled in these companies, engaged the invaders wherever they could meet them. The Rifle Factory was attacked and the party there were soon driven into the Shenandoah, where they were met by the fire of Captain Medler's company, who had crossed that river on the bridge, and between the two fires, they all perished except one, a negro named Copeland, who was taken prisoner.

At the Armory, however, where Brown commanded in person, a more determined resistance was made. Brown had told several of his prisoners in the course of the morning that he expected large re-inforcements, and when, about 12 o'clock, the company under Captain Moore, that had crossed into Maryland, was seen marching down the river, great excitement prevailed, it being supposed by the prisoners and such of the other citizens as were not aware of Captain Moore's movement and perhaps, by Brown's party, that these were the expected re-inforcements. It was soon ascertained, however, who they were and Brown, now plainly seeing that the fortunes of the day were against him, sent two of his prisoners, Archibald M. Kitzmiller and Resin Cross, under guard of two of his men, to negotiate in his name with Captain Moore for permission to vacate the place with his surviving men, without molestation. The two ambassadors proceeded with their guards towards the bridge, but, as they came near the "Gault House," several shots were fired from that building by which the two raiders were very severely wounded and put *hors-de-combat*. One of them contrived to make his way back to the Armory, but the other was unable to move, and Messrs. Kitzmiller and Cross helped him into Fouke's Hotel, where his wounds were dressed. It may well be imagined that neither of the envoys returned to captivity. Brown, finding that his doves did not come back with the olive branch, and now despairing of success, called in from the streets the survivors of his party, and picking out nine of the most prominent of his prisoners, as hostages, he retreated with his men, into a small brick building near the Armory gate called the "Engine House," taking with him his nine prisoners. A company arrived, about this time, from Martinsburg, who, with some citizens of Harper's Ferry and the surrounding country, made a rush on the Armory and released the great mass of the prisoners, not, however, without suffering some loss in wounded, caused by a galling fire kept up by the enemy from the Engine House. Brown's men had pierced the walls for musketry, and, through the holes, kept up a brisk fire by which they not only wounded the Martinsburg men and Harper's Ferrians but some Charles Town men also who had arrived a short time before. The sufferers were Messrs. Murphy, Richardson, Hammond, Dorsey, Hooper and Wollett, of Martinsburg ; Mr. Young, of Charles Town, and Mr. McCabe, of Harper's Ferry. Mr. Dorsey was very dangerously, and several of the others severely, injured. None of them, however, died from the wounds.

Before Brown's men retreated off the streets into the Engine House, two of them approached the corner of High and Shenandoah streets, where Mr. Boerly had been shot in the morning. It was then about 2 o'clock, and Mr. George Turner, a very respectable gentleman of Jefferson county, who had come to town on private business , was standing at the door of Captain Moore's house, on High street, about one hundred yards from the corner. He had just armed himself with a musket and was in the act of resting it on a board partition near the door, to take aim at one of these men, when a bullet from the rifle of one of them struck him on the shoulder, the only part of him exposed. The ball, after taking an eccentric course entered his neck and killed him almost instantly. A physician who examined him describes the wound as having been of the most singular kind, the bullet having taking a course altogether at variance with the laws supposed to regulate such projectiles. It is thought by many that the shot was not aimed at Mr. Turner, and that the man who fired it was not aware of that gentleman's being near. There were two men, named McClennen and Stedman, standing in the middle of the street, opposite Captain Moore's house. They had guns in their hands and at one of them, it is supposed, was aimed the shot that proved fatal to Mr. Turner.

After they were all housed up in their fortress, they killed another very valuable citizen, Fountain Beckham, Esq., for many years Agent of the Baltimore and Ohio Railroad company at Harper's Ferry, and long a magistrate of Jefferson county. Being a man of nervous temperament, he was, naturally, much excited by the occurrences of the day. Moreover, Heywood Shepherd, the negro shot on the bridge, the previous night,

JOHN BROWN'S HOME AND OTHER PLACES OF INTEREST.

had been his faithful servant and he was much grieved and very indignant at his death. He crept along the Railroad, under shelter of a water station which, then, stood there and peeped 'round the corner of the building at the Engine House opposite, when a bullet from one of Brown's men penetrated his heart and he died instantly. A man named Thompson, said to be Brown's son-in-law, had been taken prisoner a short time before, by the citizens and confined in Fouke's Hotel, under guard. It was the intention of the people to hand him over to the regular authorities for trial, but the death of Mr. Beckham so exasperated them that the whole current of their feelings was changed. They rushed into the hotel, seized Thompson and were dragging him out of the house to put him to death, when Miss Christina Fouke, a sister of the proprietor, with true feminine instinct, rushed into the crowd and beseeched the infuriated multitude to spare the prisoner's life. This heroic act has elicited the warmest commendations of every party, and it may be said to be the one bright spot in the history of that unfortunate day. Miss Fouke's entreaties were, however, unheeded and Thompson was hurried to the bridge where he was riddled with bullets. He, however, tried to escape by letting himself drop through the bridge into the river. He had been left for dead, but it appears he had vitality enough left to accomplish this feat. He was discovered and a shower of bullets was discharged at him. He was either killed or drowned, as he could be seen for a day or two after, lying at the bottom of the river, with his ghastly face still exhibiting his fearful death agony.

Another of the raiders named Lehman, attempted to escape from the upper end of the Armory yard, by swimming or wading the Potomac. He had been seen shortly before, conducting one of the Armory watchmen named Edward Murphy, towards the Engine House. He kept the latter between him and an armed party of citizens who were stationed on a hill near the Armory works. More than a dozen guns were raised to shoot him by the excited crowd, and no doubt both he and Murphy would have been then killed, had not Mr. Zadoc Butt induced the party not to fire, in consideration of the danger to Murphy. Lehman immediately afterwards, disappeared for a while, but soon he was seen endeavoring to escape as above mentioned. A volley was fired after him and he must have been wounded, as he lay down and threw up his arms as if surrendering. A resident of Harper's Ferry waded into the river to a rock where Lehman lay, apparently badly wounded, and deliberately shot him through the head, killing him instantly. His body, also, lay for some time where he fell.

A little before dark, Brown asked if any of the prisoners would volunteer to go out among the citizens, and induce them to cease firing on the Engine House, as they were endangering the lives of their friends who were his prisoners. He promised, on his part, that if there was no firing on his men, there should be none by them. Mr. Israel Russell undertook the dangerous duty (the danger arose from the excited state of the people who would be likely to fire on any thing seen stirring around the Engine House.) and the citizens were persuaded to stop firing, in consideration of the risk they incurred of injuring the prisoners. Like Messrs. Kitzmiller and Cross, Mr. Russell, it may well be supposed, did not return to captivity. It is certain that the citizens would, in a very short time, have disposed of Brown and his party, had not they been prevented all along from pushing the siege vigorously by a regard for the lives of their fellow-citizens who were prisoners. As it was, they had already killed, wounded or dispersed more than three-fourths of the party, and consequently the sneers that were afterwards thrown out against their bravery were altogether uncalled for and used by parties who, in the subsequent war, did not exhibit much of the reckless courage which they expected from peaceful citizens, taken by surprise, and totally at a loss for information as to the numbers and resources of their enemies.

It was now dark and the wildest terror existed in the town, especially among the friends of the killed, wounded and prisoners. It had rained some all day, and the atmosphere was raw and cold.

Now a cloudy and moonless sky hung like a pall over the scene of conflict, and on the whole, a more dismal night cannot well be imagined. Guards were stationed 'round the Engine House to prevent Brown's escape and, as forces were constantly arriving from Winchester, Frederick, Baltimore and other places, the town soon assumed quite a military appearance. The United States authorities in Washington had, in the meantime, been notified, and in the course of the night Colonel Robert E. Lee, afterwards the famous General of the Southern Confederacy, arrived with a force of United States Marines, to protect the Government interests and capture or kill the invaders. About 11 o'clock Brown again endeavored to open negotiations for a safe conduct for himself and his men out of the place. Colonel Shriver and Captain Sinn, of the Frederick troops, had a conference with him, which, however, did not result in anything satisfactory. About 7 o'clock on Tuesday morning, Colonel Lee sent, under flag of truce, Lieutenant J. E. B. Stuart, of the 1st Cavalry Regiment (afterwards so famous for his exploits as a Cavalry General in the Confederate service,) who had accompanied Colonel Lee from Washington, to summon the insurgents to surrender. Knowing the character of Brown, Colonel Lee did not hope for any success in trying to induce him to lay down his arms, and he sent Lieutenant Stuart merely through solicitude for the prisoners and a desire to try every expedient before ordering an assault and subjecting them to the danger of being injured by mistake in the melee. As anticipated, Brown stubbornly refused to surrender and, therefore, about 8 o'clock an assault was made by the marines, under Lieutenant Greene. They at first tried to break open the door with sledge hammers but failing, they picked up a ladder that lay near and with this they succeeded in making a breach. Through a narrow opening thus made Lieutenant Greene squeezed himself, but he found that the insurgents had barricaded the door with a fire engine and hose that were in the building. Over these Lieutenant Greene scrambled, followed by his men, and attacked Brown, who, with his party, was fortified behind the engine. After the marines had effected a breach and commenced rushing in, the insurgents fired on them and one of the soldiers—Luke Quinn—was mortally, and another named Rupert, slightly wounded. The former was shot through the body, and the latter in the mouth. Brown's men were all bayoneted or captured, but fortunately none of the citizen prisoners received any injury. Their escape was indeed miraculous, as it was very difficult for the marines to distinguish them from the insurgents. Brown himself was severely wounded by Lieutenant Greene and he was taken to another building where his wounds were dressed. He received a cut on the head and a sword thrust in the shoulder. Two or three survivors of his men were kept in the Engine House under guard. The bodies of the slain raiders were collected from the streets and rivers, and buried in one grave on the southern bank of the Shenandoah, about half a mile above Harper's Ferry, and the prisoners, (Brown included,) were lodged in Charles Town jail. Some had, however, escaped, and Cook had not been noticed at all in the fray since an early hour on Monday morning, when he was seen to cross over the bridge into Maryland with a few others, taking with him two horses and a wagon captured at Mr. Washington's place the previous night, and two or three slaves belonging to that gentleman. There was satisfactory evidence, however, of his having been fully implicated, and it was soon ascertained that he, Owen Brown—one of old John's sons—and others had been detailed to operate on the Maryland shore and that they had seized a schoolhouse, taken the dominie, Mr. Carrie, prisoner and driven away the pupils for the purpose of establishing at the schoolhouse a depot of arms, convenient to Harper's Ferry. It was also ascertained that they had all the day of the 17th kept up a fire from the Maryland Heights on the people of the town, and that late in the evening Cook had gotten supper at the Canal Lock-House on the Maryland side of the river. It was, moreover, supposed that finding the fate of the day against them, they had fled towards Pennsylvania. A large body of men, under Captain Edmund H. Chambers, an old citizen and a man of well known "pluck," marched towards the schoolhouse and "the Kennedy Farm," and at each place they found a large number of Sharp's rifles, pistols, swords, &c., with a considerable quantity of powder, percussion caps and equipments of various kinds. A swivel cannon, carrying a pound ball, was also discovered in a position to command the town, although it is not known that it was used during the engagement. A large number of pikes of a peculiar form and intended for the hands of the negroes, were also found. The latter were expected to turn out at the first signal, and this weapon was considered better suited for them than fire arms, especially at the commencement of the campaign. It should have been remarked before, that Brown had put into the hands of his negro prisoners some of these pikes, but up to the time of the discovery of the magazine at "the Kennedy Farm," the object of this novel weapon was not fully understood. Captain Chambers' party also found a great number of papers which tended to throw light on the conspiracy, and several hundred printed copies of a form of Provisional Government to be set up by Brown as soon as he got a footing in the South.

The constitution was adopted by a convention of colored people at Chatham, Canada, West, May 8th, 1858, and was in substance as follows:

After providing for the necessary officers of a government, it provided for trial and impeachment; for obedience, sobriety, industry and military service.

Crime of rape, like that of spying, was punished with death.

Non-slave holders were to be protected and slave holders were held as hostages, unless they gave up their slaves; valuables found were to be levied upon as act of war, and be used as safety and intelligence might direct, by order of the General.

Art. 16, read as follows, in detail : "The foregoing articles shall not be so construed as in any way to encourage the overthrow of any State government, or of the general government of the United States and looks to no dissolution of the Union, but simply to amendment and repeal, and our flag shall be the same our fathers fought under in the Revolution."

The Governor of Virginia, Henry A. Wise, had in the meantime arrived. He immediately took every precaution to secure his prisoners and the State against any attempt from the many allies Brown was supposed to have in the North. To Governor Wise he confessed the whole plan for liberating the slaves, and, indeed, he had all along communicated his intentions to his prisoners, but as we have before remarked, he kept his captives as much as possible isolated, and, in consequence, the people generally had but a vague idea of his purposes. It is true that the party at the Rifle Factory had informed Mr. Young of their object, but so many wild rumors had been started before his interview with them, and there was so much confusion generally that neither "head nor tail" could be found for the strange occurrences of the day. Governor Wise who, although he exhibited a great deal of petulance on this occasion, is certainly a brave man himself, could not refrain from expressing admiration for Brown's undaunted courage, and it is said that he pronounced him honest, truthful and brave.

The interview between these two men, of somewhat similar character, but of diametrically opposite views on politics, is said to have been very impressive. It lasted two hours and those who were present report that Brown exhibited a high order of uncultivated intellect in his interview with the highly educated and polished Governor of Virginia. It is also said that, in the course of this conversation, Brown foretold the utter destruction of Harper's Ferry, to take place in a very short time, a prophecy which, if ever uttered, has met with a terrible and literal fulfilment. This interview and the surroundings furnish a fine theme for a picture. The stern old Puritan, with his bleeding wounds and disordered dress, his long, grey beard and wild, gleaming eyes, like some prophet of old, denouncing the wrath of Heaven on a sinful generation, and the stately Governor of Virginia, reminding one of some Cavalier of Naseby or Worcester—each firm and true as the blade he carried and each a type of the noble though fanatical race from which he sprung, would certainly, make an impressive picture and the scene will, no doubt, some day occupy the genius of a future painter.

Harper's Ferry was now patroled every night by details of citizens until the execution of Brown, which took place near Charles Town, December 2nd, 1859.

A force of United States troops under Captain Seth Barton, afterwards prominent in the service of the Confederacy, was also stationed at Harper's Ferry and gradually quiet was restored.

Cook and another raider named Albert Hazlett were arrested in Pennsylvania and brought back on requisitions. This circumstance might furnish a lesson to the fanatics, who unhappily abounded on both sides of Mason and Dixon's line. To the Southern men it ought to have proved that the people of the North did not sympathize, to any great extent, with the invasion of the State of Virginia, and to the Northern men who expressed themselves as shocked at the want of mercy exhibited by the State of Virginia on this occasion, it might have shown that, among themselves were men who were ready to deliver over Brown's party to the tender mercies of the slave-holders, for the sake of a few hundred dollars reward.

Cook and another white man, named Edwin Coppie, with two negroes, named Greene and Copeland, were executed on the 16th of December in the same year, and Hazlett and Stephens, (both white,) met the same fate on the 16th of March, 1860.

Brown's trial was, of course, a mere matter of form. He took no pains to extenuate his guilt and openly avowed that he desired no favors from the State of Virginia. Two young lawyers of Boston, named Hoyt and Sennott, volunteered to defend him and they acquitted themselves creditably. The Honorable Samuel Chilton, of Washington, was employed for the defense, by John A. Andrew, of Massachusetts, afterwards Governor of that State, but, of course, nothing could save the prisoner and he was executed as above mentioned.

Brown died with unshaken fortitude and bitter as the animosity against him was, his courage or rather stoical indifference elicited the admiration, even of his enemies. Indeed, it is difficult, at the present time, to do justice to the character of this remarkable man, but, no doubt, the future historians of this country who will write when the passions that excite us have subsided or are perhaps forgotten, will class him with the Scotch Covenanters of the 17th century. It has always struck the writer that John Brown very closely resembled John Balfour, of Burly, whose character is so finely portrayed in Scott's "Old

Mortality." The same strong will and iron nerve and the same fanaticism characterized these two men and it must be said of both, (for Burly's character is taken from life,) that while no sane person could wholly approve of their actions, their bitterest enemies cannot deny a tribute of respect to their unflinching courage. The other prisoners also died bravely, and, indeed, it was a melancholy thing to see men of so much stamina loose their lives in such a foolish enterprise.

BOYER, SURVIVING JUROR.
BROWN'S X ROADS, NEAR HARPER'S FERRY.

An attempt to escape was made by Cook and Coppie on the night before their execution. By some means they succeeded in eluding the vigilance of the cell-guard and in climbing the outer wall of the prison, when they were challenged by a citizen guard who was posted outside and their further progress was prevented.

On the morning of his execution Brown bade an affectionate farewell to his fellow-captives, with the exception of Cook, whom he charged with having deceived him. It is said that he gave to each of them, with the above exception, a silver quarter of a dollar, as a memento, and told them to meet their fate courageously. He pretended not to know Hazlett at all, but this was understood by all who were present to be done in order to aid the latter whose trial had not yet come off, and who pretended that he knew nothing about Brown or the raid on Harper's Ferry. It will be remembered that he was arrested in Pennsylvania, some time after the invasion, and, of course, his defense, if he had any, would be an alibi.

Brown's wife arrived at Harper's Ferry shortly before his execution, and to her his body was delivered for burial. He was interred at North Elba, in the State of New York, where he had resided for some years. His wife was rather an intelligent woman and she did not appear to sympathize with her husband's wild notions on the subject of slavery. In conversation with a citizen of Harper's Ferry, she expressed the opinion that Brown had contemplated this or a similar raid for thirty years, although he had never mentioned the subject to her. The bodies of Cook, Coppie, Hazlet and Stevens were also delivered to friends and it is said that the two latter are buried, near the residence of a benevolent Quaker lady, in New Jersey, who deeply sympathized with them and the cause for which they suffered.

The names of the invaders, as well as could be ascertained were as follows: John Brown, Watson Brown, Oliver Brown, Owen Brown, Aaron D. Stevens, Edwin Coppie, Barclay Coppie, Albert Hazlett, John E. Cook, Stuart Taylor, William Lehman, William Thompson, John Henrie Kagi, Charles P. Tydd, Oliver Anderson, Jeremiah Anderson, 'Dolph Thompson, Dangerfield Newby, Shields Green, alias "Emperor," John Copeland and Lewis Leary, of whom the last four were negroes or mulattoes.

John Brown was, at the time of the raid, fifty-nine years old, about five feet and eleven inches in height, large-boned and muscular but not fleshy, and he gave indications of having in his youth possessed great physical strength. His hair had been a dark brown, but at this period it was gray. His beard was very long, and on the memorable day of the raid it hung in snowy waves to his breast, giving to his aquiline features a singularly wild appearance. His face was always beardless before this event. His eyes were of a dark hazel and burning with a peculiar light that gave promise of a quick temper and daring courage. His head, as it appeared to the writer, was of a conical shape, and on the whole, his physique well corresponded with the traits of his character.

There was confusion respecting the identity of his two sons, Watson and Oliver. They were mortally wounded on the 17th. One of them, a young man, apparently about twenty-three years of age, of low stature, with fair hair and blue eyes, was shot in the stomach and died, in the course of the next night, in the Engine House, while the party had still possession of it. It is said that he suffered terrible agony and that he called on his companions to put him out of pain by shooting him. His father, however, manifested no feeling on the occasion, beyond remarking, that "he must have patience; that he was dying in a good cause, and that he should meet his fate like a brave man." The other was a tall man, about six feet in height, with very black hair. He, also, as above stated, was wounded in the skirmish of the 17th, and he died next morning, after the marines had gotten possession of the Engine House. He was one of the two men who were wounded from the "Gault House." When he died, his father was a prisoner and badly wounded. On learning that one of his men had just died, he sent out to inquire if it was his son, and on being informed that it was, he manifested the same stoicism and made the similar remark as on the death of the other son. When the news reached him, he was engaged in the interview with Governor Wise. After satisfying himself as to the identity of the man who had just died, he resumed his conversation with the Governor, as if nothing had happened calculated to discompose him in the least. As before remarked, there is a doubt as to which of these two men was Watson and which was Oliver.

Owen Brown was one of those detailed to operate in Maryland. He was not in the fray, but made his escape and was never captured. We cannot, therefore, give a description of his personal appearance.

Aaron D. Stevens was a remarkably fine looking young man, of about thirty years of age. He was about five feet and ten inches in height, heavily built, and of great symmetry of form. His hair was black and his eyes, of dark hazel, had a very penetrating glance. He was said to be a desperate character, and as it was known that he had suggested to Brown the murder of the prisoners and the firing of the village, there was greater animosity felt towards him than any of the others, except, perhaps, old Brown himself and Cook. He received several wounds in the skirmish and it was thought he could not survive them. In consequence of these injuries, he was one of the last put on trial and executed. He was said to be a believer in Spiritualism. He was the one who was so badly wounded from the "Gault House" and who was taken to Fouke's hotel. Had he not been disabled, it is to be feared, from what is reported of him, that a massacre of Brown's prisoners would have taken place, on his recommendation. Whatever his crimes may have been, it is certain that he was a man of iron nerve. While he lay, helplessly wounded at Fouke's hotel, a crowd of armed citizens gathered around him and it was with the utmost difficulty that a few of the less excited people succeeded in saving his life. One citizen put the muzzle of his loaded gun to Stevens' head, with the expressed determination to kill him instantly. Stevens was then unable to move a limb, but he fixed his terrible eyes on the would-be murderer, and by the sheer force of their magnetism or whatever you may choose to call their mysterious power, he compelled the man to lower his gun and spare his life. To this day, the citizen avers that he cannot account for the irresistible fascination that bound him, as with a spell.

Edwin Coppie (or Coppie) was a young man, aged about twenty-four years, about five feet, six inches in height, compactly built and of a florid complexion. He was a very handsome youth and for various reasons great sympathy was felt for him by many. He was not wounded in the engagement, but taken prisoner by the marines from the Engine House. He had come from Iowa, where his widowed mother, a pious old lady belonging to the Society of "Friends," resided. He had been, for a long time, in the employ of a Mr. Thomas Gwynn, residing near Tipton, Cedar county, in the above mentioned State. Mr. Gwynn was a farmer and merchant and Coppie assisted him as a farm laborer and "help" around his store. Mr. Gwynn was much attached to him and came to Charles Town for his remains, which he took with him to Iowa.

After Coppie's conviction, a petition, numerously signed, was forwarded to the Governor of Virginia, requesting executive clemency in his case. It was not successful, however, and he was executed, as before mentioned. In conversation with a citizen of Harper's Ferry, who interviewed him in his cell, he remarked that when he left his home in Iowa he had no intention of entering on any expedition like the one against Virginia, but he confessed that his object was to induce slaves to leave their masters and to aid them to escape.

Of Barclay Coppie little is known beyond the fact of his having been Edwin's brother. He was with Owen Brown and Cook, on the Maryland side, and was never captured. It is said that he was killed some years ago in Missouri, by a railroad accident.

Albert Hazlett, of Pennsylvania, was a man of about five feet and eleven inches in height, raw-boned and muscular. His hair was red and his eyes were of a muddy brown and of a very unpleasant expression. He was very roughly dressed on the day of the raid, and in every sense of the word, he looked like "an ugly customer." He made his escape from Harper's Ferry on the evening of the 17th, about the time that Brown withdrew his force into the Engine House, but he was afterwards captured in Pennsylvania and executed with Stevens. His age was about thirty-three years.

John E. Cook was a native of Connecticut, and he, was a young man, of about twenty-eight years of age, about five feet and eight inches in height, but, as he stooped a good deal, he did not appear to be so tall. He had fair hair and bright blue eyes and was, on the whole, quite an intelligent looking man. He had, as before stated, resided several years at Harper's Ferry, and had become acquainted with all the young men of the place, by whom he was regarded as a pleasant companion, and had married a respectable lady there. He was highly connected and the Governor of Indiana, (Willard,) was his brother-in-law, having married Cook's sister. On his trial, Mr. Voorhees, now so prominent in the West as a politician, and then widely known as an able criminal lawyer, made a speech for the defense which is regarded as one of his best efforts.

Little is known, for certain, of Stuart Taylor. Some contend that he was a man of medium size and very dark complexion, while others believe that he was a red haired young man who was bayoneted by the marines in the Engine House and dragged dead from that building at the same time that Brown was removed. The writer is inclined to the latter opinion and he thinks that those who favor the former confound him with a man named Anderson, of whom we will soon speak at some length.

William Lehman, who was killed on a rock in the Potomac, while endeavoring to escape, was quite a young man, with jet black hair and a very florid complexion. The killing of this young man was, under all the circumstances of the case, an act of great barbarity, as he had made signs of a desire to surrender. The man who shot him was but a temporary resident of Harper's Ferry and belonged originally to Martinsburg. His name we will omit for the sake of his posterity.

William Thompson, who was shot on the bridge, was a man apparently of about thirty years of age, of medium size but of great symmetry of form. His complexion was fair and he gave indications of being a man of a very pleasant disposition. He was well known to many in the neighborhood of "the Kennedy farm," and he was very popular in the vicinity. The killing of this man, also, was unnecessary, but some palliation may be found for it on account of the excitement caused by the death of Mr. Beckham.

John, or as he was sometimes called, Henrie Kagi, is said to have been a remarkably fine looking man with a profusion of black hair and a flowing beard of the same color. He was about thirty years of age, tall and portly, and he did not display the same ferocity that the others exhibited. He was "Secretary of

DISTINGUISHED PEOPLE CONNECTED WITH JOHN BROWN'S TRIAL.

War," under Brown's Provisional Government and he held the rank of Captain. He is supposed to have been a native of Ohio. He was killed in the Shenandoah near the Rifle Factory.

Of Charles P. Tydd little is known. It is said that before the raid he used to peddle books through the neighborhood of Harper's Ferry. As far as ascertained he did not appear in the fight, but escaped from Maryland to parts unknown. It is said he was a native of Maine.

Respecting the identity of Oliver and Jeremiah Anderson, there is a doubt as in the case of the Browns. One of them was killed by the marines, but what became of the other is unknown.

The man who was killed was about thirty years of age, of middle stature, with very black hair and dark complexion. He was supposed by some to be a Canadian mulatto. He is also, as before remarked, confounded by many with Stuart Taylor. He received three or four bayonet stabs in the breast and stomach and when he was dragged out of the engine house to the flagged walk in front, he was yet alive and vomiting gore from internal hemorrhage. While he was in this condition, a farmer from some part of the surrounding country came up and viewed him in silence, but with a look of concentrated bitterness. Not a word did he speak, thinking no doubt, that no amount of cursing could do justice to his feelings. He passed on to another part of the yard and did not return for a considerable time. When he came back, Anderson was still breathing and the farmer thus addressed him : "Well, it takes you a h–ll of a long time to die." If Anderson had vitality enough left in him to hear this soothing remark, it must have contributed greatly to smooth his way to the unknown land of disembodied spirits. The writer heard from very good authority, that another and still greater barbarity was practiced towards this man while he was in the death agony. Some brute in human shape, it is said, squirted tobacco juice and dropped his quid in the dying man's eye. The writer did not see the latter occurrence, but it is related by witnesses of undoubted veracity. After death, also, this man Anderson appeared to have been picked out for special honors and the most marked attentions. Some physicians of Winchester, Virginia, fancied him as a subject for dissection, and *nem. con.* they got possession of his body. In order to take him away handily, they procured a barrel and tried to pack him into it. Head foremost, they rammed him in, but they could not bend his legs so as to get them into the barrel with the rest of his body. In their endeavors to accomplish this feat, they strained so hard that the man's bones or sinews, fairly cracked. The praise-worthy exertions of those sons of Galen, in the cause of science and humanity elicited the warmest expressions of approval from the spectators. The writer does not know what disposition they finally made of him.

Dolph Thompson was quite a boy and he appeared to be an unwilling participator in the transaction. He was seen by not more than two or three citizens and it is supposed that he escaped early on the 17th. He had fair hair and a florid complexion.

Dangerfield Newby was a tall, well built mulatto, aged about thirty years, with a pleasing face. He was shot and killed at the Arsenal gate, by somebody in Mrs. Butler's house opposite, about 11 o'clock A. M., on Monday, and he lay where he fell until the afternoon of Tuesday. The bullet struck him in the lower part of the neck and went down into his body, the person who shot him being in a position more elevated than the place where Newby was standing. Mr. Jacob Bajeant, of Harper's Ferry, claims the credit of having fired the fatal shot and the people generally accord him the honor. From the relative positions of the parties, the size of the bullet or some other circumstances, the hole in his neck was very large and the writer heard a party remark that he believed a smoothing iron had been shot into him. Shortly after his death, a hog came rooting about him, apparently unconscious, at first, that it was Lord 'of Creation that lay there. The hog, after a while, paused and looked attentively at the body, then snuffed around it and, finally, put its snout to the man's face. Suddenly, the brute was seized with a panic and with bristles erect and drooping tail, it scampered away, as if for life. This display of sensibility was very creditable to that hog, but soon a drove of the same species crowded round the dead man, none of which appeared to be actuated by the same generous impulse as the first.—The pertinacity with which death holds on to a dead African is so well known, that it has become proverbial, but, the King of Terrors himself could not exceed those hogs in zealous attention to the defunct Newby. They tugged away at him with might and main and the writer saw one run its snout into the wound and drag out a stringy substance of some kind which he is not anatomist enough to call by its right name. It appeared to be very long or very elastic, as it reached fully three yards, from the man's neck, one end being in the hog's mouth and the other some where in the man's body. This circumstance could not fail to improve the flavor and enhance the value of pork, at

Harper's Ferry, the next winter. On Tuesday evening after Brown was made a prisoner, and the people were somewhat relieved from the terror of a more extensive and dangerous invasion, a citizen of Harper's Ferry, who had not had a chance to distinguish himself, in the skirmish on Monday, fired a charge of shot into the dead body of Newby, a feat which, no doubt, tended to exalt him, at least in his own opinion. Like Kirkpatrick, at the murder of the Red Comyn, he thought he would "make sicker," and guard against any possibility of the dead man's reviving. The citizen referred to was somewhat under the influence of whiskey, but the writer saw another, apparently sober, and a man of excellent standing in the community, kick the dead man in the face, and, on the whole, great a crime as the invasion of the place was, and natural as the animosity towards the invaders should be considered, it must be confessed that the treatment the lifeless bodies of those wretched men received from many of the infuriated populace, was far from being creditable to the actors or to human nature, generally.

Shields Greene, *alias* Emperor, was a negro of the blackest hue, small in stature and very active in his movements. He seemed to be very officious, flitting about from place to place, and he was, evidently, conscious of his own extra importance in the enterprize. It is supposed that it was he who killed Mr. Boerly. He was said to be a resident of the State of New York, but little is known, for certain, about him. He was very insulting to Brown's prisoners, constantly presenting his rifle and threatening to shoot them. He was aged about thirty years.

John Copeland was a mulatto, of medium size and about twenty-five years of age. He was a resident of Oberlin, Ohio, where he carried on the carpenter business for some years.

Lewis Leary, a mulatto, was mortally wounded at the Rifle Factory and died in a carpenter's shop, on "the island." He was a young man, but his personal appearance cannot be minutely described, as when captured he was suffering great agony and, of course, did not present his natural appearance. He also had resided in Oberlin, and his trade was that of harness-making.

A negro man, whom Mr. Washington had hired from a neighbor and who had been taken prisoner with Mr. Washington the previous night, was drowned while endeavoring, to escape from his captors.—He was an unwilling participant in the transaction and no blame was attached to him by the people.

Heywood Shepherd, the first man killed by Brown's party

was a very black negro, aged about forty-four years. He was uncommonly tall, measuring six feet and five inches, and he was a man of great physical strength. He was free, but in order to comply with a law then existing in Virginia, he acknowledged "Squire" Beckham as his master. The relations of master and slave, however, existed only in name between them, and Heywood accumulated a good deal of money and owned some property in Winchester. He was a married man and he left several children.

It is supposed by many that the killing of this man, alone, prevented a general insurrection of the negroes, for some of the farmers in the neighborhood say that they noticed an unusual excitement among their slaves on the Sunday before the raid. If it be true that the negroes knew anything of the intended attack, it is probable they were deterred from taking a part by seeing one of their own race the first man sacrificed.

Thomas Boerly, the second man killed, was a native of the county of Roscommon, in Ireland. As before noticed, he was a man of great physical strength and he was noted for "pluck." He measured about six feet in height, and weighed over two hundred pounds. He was a blunt, straight-forward man in his dealings and he was very popular on account of his love of fun and from that somewhat inexplicable tendency of human nature, to pay respect to the purely accidental quality of personal strength. Many years before he encountered and fought an equally powerful man, named Joseph Graff, who, at that time, resided at Harper's Ferry. The fight was conducted in the old border style of "rough and tumble," including biting and gouging. Night, alone, terminated the encounter and the combatants parted, with their mutual respect greatly augmented and with a great accession of glory to them both. The admirers of each party claimed a victory for their champion, but the combatants wisely divided the laurels and never again jeopardized their reputations by renewing the contest. Mr. Boerly's age was about forty-three years. He was married and he left three children. The State of Virginia granted a small pension to his widow, but the war breaking out shortly after, she received no portion of it, until, at the restoration of peace, her claim was brought to the notice of the authorities. She has since been paid punctually. Mr. Boerly kept a grocery and he was in very comfortable circumstances.

George Turner, the third man killed, was a fine looking man, aged about forty years. It is said that he was educated at West

Point and that he was distinguished for great polish and refinement of manners. He was unmarried and left a great deal of property. He was a native of Jefferson county, Virginia.

Fountain Beckham, the forth man killed, was, like the others, a tall, powerfully built man. His age was about sixty years. He was a native of Culpepper county, Virginia, and a brother of Armstead Beckham, heretofore mentioned as Master Armorer. As before stated, he had been for many years a magistrate of the county and the agent of the Baltimore & Ohio railroad company, at Harper's Ferry. At the time of his death, he was Mayor of the town. He was a widower and two sons and a daughter survived him. Mr. Beckham was in many respects a remarkable man. It is said that he was the best magistrate that Jefferson county ever possessed, his decisions being always given with a view rather to the justice than the law of the cases, and in many instances being marked with great shrewdness and soundness of judgment. On the other hand, he was sometimes very whimsical and some amusing scenes used to be enacted between him and Heywood. "The Squire" would frequently give unreasonable orders to his servant, who never hesitated on such occasions to refuse obedience, and it was no uncommon thing to see Heywood starting out from the railroad office with his bundle on his back en route for Winchester, swearing that he would never serve "the Squire" another day. He never proceeded very far, however, before he was overtaken by a message from "the Squire" bringing proposals for peace and Heywood never failed to return. Notwithstanding their frequent rows, a strong attachment existed between these two men through life, and in death they were not separated. Mr. Beckham was very respectably connected. His sister was the wife of Mr. Stubblefield, so long superintendent of the Armory, and his niece, Miss Stubblefield, was married to Andrew Hunter, of Charles Town, one of the most eminent lawyers of Virginia. Mr. Beckham's wife was the daughter of Colonel Stevenson, of Harper's Ferry, and it will thus be seen that he was connected with many of the most influential families in "the Northern Neck." Mr. Beckham's death was mourned as a public loss, for, with many oddities of manner, he was a very kind hearted man and a good citizen.

The nine citizens confined as hostages in the Engine House were as follows: Colonel Lewis W. Washington, and John Allstadt, planters; John E. P. Dangerfield, paymaster's clerk; A. M. Ball, master machinist; Benjamin Mills, master armorer; John Donohoo, assistant agent of the Baltimore and Ohio Railroad at Harper's Ferry ; Terence O'Byrne, a farmer residing in Washington county, Maryland ; Israel Russell, merchant of Harper's Ferry, and a Mr. Schoppe, of Frederick City, Maryland, who happened to be at Harper's Ferry that day on a business visit.

Colonel Lewis W. Washington was at that time a very fine looking man of about fifty years of age, with that unmistakable air that always accompanies a man of true patrician birth and education. He was the soul of hospitality and Cook used to visit him for the ostensible purpose of contending with him in pistol-shooting, an accomplishment for which they were both famous. Mr. Washington on these occasions used to exhibit the sword and other relics of his great namesake and kinsman and thus it was that Cook and his companions gained such an intimate knowledge of his household arrangements, as enabled them to discover where the relics were stored and to capture him without difficulty. Cook was always hospitably entertained whenever he visited Mr. Washington and the ingratitude manifested towards that gentleman was, perhaps, the worst feature of the whole transaction and it is not to be excused for the moral effect that the capture might be expected to secure. Mr. Washington, it is said, exhibited on this occasion a great deal of the dignity and calmness which characterized his illustrious kinsman and his fellow captives yet speak of his remarkable coolness under the trying circumstances of his situation.

Mr. Washington, in his evidence before the select committee of the United States Senate, John Sherman, O., Wm. A. Howard, Mich., and Congressman Oliver, Missouri, appointed to inquire into the outrage, gave a description of his capture by the party. He described them as having consisted of Stevens, Cook, Tydd, Taylor and the negro, Shields Greene. Another named Merriam was supposed to have been about the premises, but he was not seen by Mr. Washington. It may be remarked that Merriam, although he is known to have been connected with the enterprize, was not seen to figure at Harper's Ferry and what became of him is unknown. It is understood that he was an Englishman by birth and that he was, in early life, a protege of Lady Byron, widow of the celebrated poet. Mr. Washington was one of those who disagreed with the author, as to the identity of Stuart Taylor. In the writer's opinion, Anderson and not Taylor was the man who accompanied the party to Mr. Washington's house.

That gentleman had several narrow escapes from death, while in the hands of "the Philistines." About the time Mr. Beckham was killed. Brown was sitting on the fire engine, near the Engine House door, rifle in hand, apparently watching an opportunity to make a good shot. Mr. Washington noticed him fingering his rifle abstractedly and like a person touching the strings of a violin, and, being somewhat struck by the comicality of the idea, he approached Brown for the purpose of inquiring if he had ever learned to play the fiddle. We may well imagine the answer the stern Puritan would have returned, had there been time to propound the question. As Mr. Washington came near Brown, a bullet from the outside whistled immediately over the head of the latter, penetrating the handle of an axe that was suspended on the engine and passed through Mr. Washington's beard into the wall near him, sprinkling brick-dust all over him. Brown coolly remarked: "That was close" and Mr. Washington postponed his question, thereby consigning posterity to ignorance on the momentous question—whether or not John Brown played on the fiddle. Mr. Washington, deeming it prudent to leave that neighborhood, moved a little to one side, when he entered into conversation with Mr. Mills, another of the prisoners. Their faces were not four inches apart, yet through this narrow passage another bullet whistled, and the friends, finding one place as safe as another, continued their conversation.

Mr. Allstadt is a gentleman of about sixty years of age, of very unassuming manners and popular for his amiable disposition. He, also, was examined before the Senate committee and gave a lively picture of his adventures while a prisoner.

John E. I. Dangerfield is a gentleman of about fifty-five years of age and of a delicate constitution. He bore up very well, however, and when he was released by the marines his physical strength had not given way, as his friends feared it would. He now resides in North Carolina.

Armstead M. Ball was at that time a man of about forty-six years of age. He was very corpulent but, notwithstanding his great bulk, his health was delicate. He died in June, 1861, of apoplexy. As before said, he was a man of wonderful mechanical ingenuity. He invented a rifling machine which was used for several years in the Armory and was regarded as a very ingenious piece of mechanism.

Benjamin Mills was a man of about fifty years of age at the time of the Brown raid, low in stature but muscular and active. He returned, as before stated, to Harrodsburg, Kentucky, where he had formerly resided.

STORER COLLEGE.

BATTLEFIELD MARKER.

John Donohoo is quite a good looking man of about forty years of age. He is a native of Ireland, but he emigrated at a very early age to this country. He resided many years at Harper's Ferry, where he was highly respected for his integrity and business qualifications. He is now a merchant in Leitersburg, Washington county, Maryland.

Terence O'Byrne is a man of about fifty-five years of age. He is in very comfortable circumstances and resides near the "Kennedy farm," where, unfortunately for him, he became well known to Brown and his party. Mr. O'Byrne was examined before the Senate committee and testified that the party who captured him was composed of Cook, Tydd and Lehman.

Israel Russell is a man of sixty years of age. He was for many years a magistrate of Jefferson county, and was always greatly respected. He now resides in Loudoun county, Virginia.

Of Mr. Schoppe little is known at Harper's Ferry. As before stated, he resides in Frederick city, Maryland.

It is somewhat remarkable that the above mentioned gentlemen who were prisoners displayed little or no vindictiveness towards Brown. The writer has frequently noticed, in conversation with these men, that they invariably dwelt on his extraordinary courage and that the animosity which it was natural they should feel, on account of the great danger to which Brown exposed them, was lost in their admiration for his daring though misguided bravery. Mr. Donohoo visited Brown in prison and, very much to his credit, exhibited towards his fallen foe a generosity characteristic of the man himself and the gallant nation of his birth.

This is "Brown's Raid," so called, an invasion which may be considered as the commencement of our civil war. It, of course, created intense excitement all over the land and the feeling then aroused never entirely subsided until the election of Mr. Lincoln, in November, 1860, renewed the quarrel on a greater scale. As before noticed, a select committee of the United States Senate was appointed to investigate the occurrence and the following gentlemen testified before it: John Allstadt, A. M. Ball, George W. Chambers, Lynn F. Currie, Andrew Hunter, A. M. Kitzmiller, Dr. John D. Starry, John C. Unseld, Lewis W. Washington and Daniel Whelan, all of Harper's Ferry or its neighborhood. Many gentlemen from the Northern and Western States also, who were supposed to be sympathizers with Brown, were called on to testify. Prominent among these were John A. Andrew, a lawyer of Boston, afterwards Governor of

Massachusetts, and Joshua Giddings, a leading anti-slavery man of Ohio, and for many years a member of Congress from that State. Nothing, however, was elicited to prove that any considerable number of people from the Free States knew of the contemplated raid and all unprejudiced minds were convinced that the knowledge of it was mostly confined to Brown and the party that accompanied him on the expedition. Thus Harper's Ferry enjoys the distinction of having been the scene of the first act of our fearful drama.

"John Brown was born in Torrington, Conn., in 1800, and was descended from an ancestor who landed at Plymouth Rock from the Mayflower. His youth and early manhood were spent in Ohio and it was during those early years, when his character was forming, that he conceived a disgust for military life and a detestation for slavery. His education was religious and he contemplated entering the Calvinistic ministry, but hesitated owing to impaired eyesight. In 1840 he embarked in the wool trade in Ohio, after some disastrous business transactions in Pennsylvania, and 1846 he removed with his family to Springfield, Mass., where he opened a wool warehouse and conducted business until 1849. An eastern trust—there were trusts even in those days—forced him out of business and stripped him of everything. He then began the reclamation of a wild tract of land at North Elba in the Adirondacks, given him by Gerrit Smith, and at the same time he became the active friend of a colony of southern negroes which Mr. Smith had planted there. In 1855 he went to Lykins county, Kan., where four of his sons had taken up claims near the village of Ossawattomie and where on account of their anti-salvery opinions they were harassed and plundered by bands of pro-slavery men from Missouri.

Kansas was then in the wildest disorder; continual strife and bloodshed were of daily occurence between the Free-soilers.

He was married twice and the father of 21 children.

Near Pasadena, Cal., 5000 miles above the sea is the grave of Owen Brown, his son and trusted Lieutenant at Harper's Ferry, who escaped thither. The occupant of the house is Jason, his brother, 73 years of age. The place is called Mt. Lowe. Owen and his brother made a trail to the peak above, called Brown's peak, in honor of them. It is kept in repair for tourists. Besides Jason, Ruth, Anna, Sarah and Helen live in this state and Salmon, a son, resides in Oregon. John Brown, Jr., died in Sandusky, O., a short time ago. It is said of John Brown's raid, "Time has given it a fuller perspective and a coloring and that he stands forth a shining example of self-sacrifice and heroism. He was a man of extremes. He had a Quaker's hatred of war, yet he freely embarked in it. He practiced piety, yet he approved of and probably took a leading part in the horrible five-fold murder (Doyles and his two sons, Wilkinson and Sherman in Kansas.) He dearly loved his family, yet he had no hesitancy in exposing them to death. He was a dreamer, yet a man of action."

The Annals of Harper's Ferry concludes its war episode with this eloquent tribute to the hero of Ossawattomie:

We will conclude this imperfect account of "Harper's Ferry during the war," by commenting on a fact which, although it may be accidental, has certainly a strong significance for a reflecting mind. Of all the government buildings in the Armory enclosure before the war, the only one that has escaped destruction during that fearful struggle is John Brown's famous Engine House. Of the occurrence that gave fame to this little building, there can be only one opinion—that it was a gross violation of law for which the aggressors paid a just, legal penalty. On the other hand, it must be admitted that slavery was not only an evil but a disgrace to the Model Republic of modern times and this civilized century. Who knows, then, but that providence selected this enthusiast as its instrument in removing that anomalous stigma of slavery from the State that boasts of having given birth to Washington, and of containing his ashes, and from this whole nation that can now, at least, truly call itself "the land of the free." The preservation of this little building is, certainly, somewhat singular, and is takes but a small stretch of imagination to prophesy that it will be the Mecca to which many a pilgrim of this and other lands will in future years journey, as to a shrine consecrated to liberty. John Brown was a violator of law and, as before remarked, he suffered a just punishment for his invasion of Virginia and his attempt at exciting a servile insurrection, but he was, certainly, honest, and it must be admitted that he gave the strongest proofs of sincerity when he sacrificed his life and the lives of his children for the cause he advocated. Of course, many will dissent from this opinion of slavery, especially in the South, if indeed, any considerable number will peruse these unpretending pages, but all must admit that John Brown's raid caused a revolution, the most extraordinary in the annals of this globe, and one that showed the most unmistakable signs of Providential interposition. As lately as October, 1859, the institution of slavery bade fair to last as long as the eternal mountains, and not only that, but to spread over most of the vast regions of the Mississippi Valley, as yet unsettled by the Caucasian. It was hedged in and protected by every safeguard which legislation, state or national, could build around it, and in the South it was cherished with an idolatry surpassing that of any pagan nation for its gods—an idolatry so fanatical and fierce as to preclude any safety to the person rash enough to doubt the divine origin of the institution. In the North there was a very strong party who cherished it, for political purposes and for that anomalous sentiment in the human heart which glorifies, even in a republic, an aristocracy either real or pretended. The Congress of the United States had, a few years before, passed the "Fugitive Slave Law," an enactment the most disgraceful of any in the annals of legislation, and one which showed the depth to which the roots of this monstrous evil and iniquity had sunk into the hearts of the American people, as, of course, it could not have passed without a very strong support from the non-slaveholding States. The hopes of the slave and the lover of liberty were dead and beyond the least prospect of resurrection when an humble man, without wealth, education or influence, but moved by a spirit which must now be believed to have emanated from heaven, with twenty-one others, equally humble, came, and in one short hour, sapped the deeply laid foundations of this structure, until it tumbled to destruction within four years. We may, therefore, well consider our revolution a dispensation of a just providence and the mission of John Brown as heaven-directed, and we will venture to prophesy that before many years a monument to the memory of that missionary of freedom will stand on the site of his famous Engine House, or on the spot near Charles Town, from which his soul commenced to "march on"—literally to heaven, and figuratively to the emancipation of four millions of the human race. A native of a land that has for seven hundred years groaned under the iron rule of a foreign oppressor, and one who with his mother's milk drew in a hatred of tyranny and a corresponding love for the martyrs of freedom in every land, the author suggests the erection of this monument and he predicts that in a short time, there will be no man prouder of it or the hero it will commemorate than the gallant Virginian who, though he fought fiercely against liberty, did so through the errors of his education alone, for he is in reality among the most chivalrous of mankind. A little experience of the benefits of the abolition of slavery, even to the white race, has already had a marked effect on the feelings of the people of Virginia, and it is evident that the next generation will look with horror and contempt on the relic of barbarism for which their fathers so persistently contended. "*Exegi monumentum are perennius*" might well be the legend on the "John Brown column," for neither brass nor marble will endure as long as the work he has accomplished, and the good deeds that live after the man—acts which, in their consequences, effect beneficially remote posterity, are the performer's proudest and most lasting monument. There is a remarkable illustration of this truth at Harper's Ferry, for not a fourth of a mile from the Engine House, where only twelve years ago the first blow was struck at the fetters of the American slave, already towers "Storer College," an institution originally endowed by the munificence of a private citizen for the education of the freedmen, and every year a class of graduates, of both sexes, leave its halls to impart in turn to their less fortunate brethren, in distant localities, the blessings of a liberal, Christian education. This institution is a corallary of John Brown's idea and it is the noblest monument that could be erected to perpetuate his fame. It, moreover, affords a practical and complete refutation of the calumny which asserted the incapacity of the negro mind for receiving instruction, and the yearly commencement exhibitions at this infant college, even now, compare favorably with those of the oldest and proudest seminaries in the land. It is gratifying to see that its merits are attracting attention from the wealthy and munificent all over the country, and that bequests and donations for its benefit are being made by the benevolent in various sections. As the field in which this institution has to labor is co-extensive with the late slave states and as the numbers seeking its advantages are almost beyond calculation, we would invite to it the attention of the many philanthropists which our country, happily, possesses, although it frequently happens that their charities are not directed to the worthiest objects."

❧ CHARLES TOWN, ❧

the place of the execution of John Brown and his confederates, is the county seat of Jefferson County, and is eight miles from Harper's Ferry, with which it is connected by pike and the Valley Branch of the B. & O. R. R. It is situated upon a high and beautiful undulating ground, 580 feet above the sea and commands a varied and beautiful scenery—North Mountains on the

RESIDENCE OF COL. JOHN GIBSON, OF CHARLES TOWN.

west and the Blue Ridge mountain and Harper's Ferry gap on the east, eliciting the expression from John Brown on his way to the scaffold, "that it was a beautiful country."

The town was laid out by Charles Washington, brother of General George Washington, 1786. It contains 3000 inhabitants, with social advantages unsurpassed by any town of its size elsewhere, and is what you might call an old aristocratic southern town. A great many of the descendants of our illustrious forefathers, who made the early history of our country, still live here, though their magnificent homes have in some cases fallen in the hands of northerners who have come amongst them to live and in many cases have married their daughters also.

Slave quarters and other evidences of anti-bellum days can still be traced here.

The residence of Col. John Gibson is built upon the spot of the execution. He is a typical southern gentleman of ante-bellum days of that section, chivalrous, courteous and honest.

It was these virtues so conspicuously possessed by the opposing men of the late war that easily led the writer up to the conclusion that the clash of arms was due to their different educations.

Lee showed great courtesy to Brown after his capture and he in return spoke of the greatness of the southern people, save slavery. Horace Greely, the great abolitionist, went on Jefferson Davis' bond and gave him freedom, and Grant offered his sword to President Johnson before one of the rebels should be hurt. In view of these facts, then, is not a foreign war a blessing, so that all the citizens of all sections can be restored to the same footing —a regeneration of the nation, a re-baptism into citizenship? The court house made famous by the trial of Brown and his men is still here with other places made interesting by this and other events.

"In the beauty of the lilies Christ was born across the sea,
With a glory in his bosom that transfigures you and me.
As he died to make men holy, let us die to make men free,
    While God is marching on."
            —*Battle Hymn of the Republic.*

ANTIETAM AVENUE LEADING INTO SHARPSBURG.

ANTIETAM.

ANTIETAM is a beautiful rolling section of country, lying at the foot of the Blue Ridge system. Its fields are green and waving, with a Quaker's quietness reigning around, and possessing no marks of the great struggle for human liberty, save only what man has placed there since as memorials. It is called Antietam from the creek which traverses it, which first gave its beautiful Indian name to the line of battle and afterwards to the whole territory over which the battle spread. It is reached by pike some twelve miles over a level and beautiful farming country by Shepherdstown, or mountain road through primitive forests, across murmuring brooks and by cool, gurgling springs. To go one way and return the other gives you a circuit of twenty-five miles' drive of beautiful and varied scenery and many interesting historical points, viz: the old southern town of Shepherdstown, Lee's headquarters on Shepherdstown road, Sharpsburg and Antietam battlefields, by Reno's monument, Turner's and Crampton's Gaps and Horseshoe monument, and residence of Geo. Alford Townsend, better known as "Gath," in South Mountain, Kennedy Farm and John Brown's rendezvous, in "Sample's Manor." In the North the battlefield is known as Antietam, in the South, as Sharpsburg, the reason being, that the Confederate line passed through the latter place toward the river.

The residence of Hon. Jacob H. Grove, a brick house slightly elevated, on southwest corner of public square, is marked as the place where Lee held a conference with Longstreet and D. H. Hill, but his headquarters were in tents pitched in a grove on

ANTIETAM CEMETERY—SHARPSBURG.

the right of the Shepherdstown road, just outside of town. Sharpsburg is a shady little town of some 1000 inhabitants, nestling in the hollow of the surrounding hills, and is improved by battlefield roads through and around it, being the intention of the Government later to join them south of the town. In view of

MONUMENTS TO WAR CORRESPONDENTS, AND HOME OF GEORGE ALFRED TOWNSOND, ESQ., OF SOUTH MOUNTAIN.

this circumstance then, would it not be fitting and in the whole appropriate that the center of the town that widens into a public square, be set off by a fitting memorial perpetuating the great issue upon which this bloody battle hinged, the Emancipation Proclamation. The improvements of the battlefield all around the town will naturally force some ornamentation of this square, and a step of this kind by its citizens, I think, would not be out of order and very proper. An agitation of the subject would hurt nothing and quite likely produce something in the long run.

Previous to this battle, the day was a bright one for the Confederates and a dark one for the Union forces. Lee crossed into Maryland at White's Ford and took the direction of Frederick city in an invasion of the north. McClellan, just reinstated into command, followed closely but cautiously upon his heels and brought him to an engagement on the banks of the far-famed Antietam.

Had the people of Maryland responded to the address of Gen. Lee and the battle been a Confederate triumph, then no doubt our rock of Union and Liberty would have been blasted forever.

MONUMENTS ERECTED UPON THE BATTLEFIELD BY VARIOUS REGIMENTS OF THE UNION ARMY.

ANTIETAM.

"HEADQUARTERS ARMY OF NORTHERN VIRGINIA,
"NEAR FREDERICK, MD., September 8th, 1862.

"*To the People of Maryland:*

"It is right that you should know the purpose that has brought the army under my command within the limits of your State, so far as that purpose concerns yourselves.

"The people of the Confederate States have long watched with the deepest sympathy the wrongs and outrages that have been inflicted upon the citizens of a commonwealth allied to the States of the South by the strongest social, political, and commercial ties, and reduced to the condition of a conquered province.

"Under the pretense of supporting the Constitution, but in violation of its most valuable provisions, your citizens have been arrested and imprisoned, upon no charge and contrary to all the forms of law.

"A faithful and manly protest against this outrage, made by a venerable and illustrious Marylander, (Roger B. Taney,) to whom in better days no citizen appealed for right in vain, was treated with scorn and contempt.

"The government of your chief city has been usurped by armed strangers; your Legislature has been dissolved by the unlawful arrest of its members; freedom of the press and of speech has been suppressed; words have been declared offenses by an arbitrary decree of the Federal Executive, and citizens ordered to be tried by military commissions for what they may dare to speak.

"Believing that the people of Maryland possess a spirit too lofty to submit to such a government, the people of the South have long wished to aid you in throwing off this foreign yoke, to enable you again to enjoy the inalienable rights of freemen, and restore the independence and sovereignty of your State.

"This, citizens of Maryland, is our mission, so far as you are concerned. No restraint upon your free will is intended. No intimidation will be allowed within the limits of this army, at least. We know no enemies among you, and will protect all of you in every opinion.

"It is for you to decide your destiny freely and without constraint. This army will respect your choice, whatever it may be; and, while the Southern people will rejoice to welcome you to your natural position among them, they will only welcome you when you come of your own free will.

"R. E. LEE, General Commanding."

Lee's Famous Lost Order at Frederick.

"HEADQUARTERS ARMY OF NORTHERN VIRGINIA,
"September 9th, 1862.

"The army will resume its march to-morrow, taking the Hagerstown road; General Jackson's command will form the advance, and, after passing Middletown, with such portion as he may select, take the route toward Sharpsburg, cross the Potomac at the most convenient point, and by Friday night take possession of Baltimore & Ohio Railroad, capture such of the enemy as may be at Martinsburg and intercept such as may attempt to escape from Harper's Ferry. Gen. Longstreet's command will pursue the same road as far as Boonsboro, where it will halt with the reserve supply and baggage trains of the army.

Gen. McLaws with his own division and that of Gen. R. H. Anderson will follow Gen. Longstreet ; on reaching Middletown, he will take the route to Harper's Ferry and by Friday morning possess himself of the Maryland Heights, and endeavor to capture the enemy at Harper's Ferry and vicinity.

General Walker with his division, after accomplishing the object in which he is now engaged, will cross the Potomac at Cheek's ford, ascend its right bank to Lovettsville, take possession of Loudoun Heights if practicable by Friday morning, Key's Ford on his left, and the road between the end of the mountain and the Potomac on his right. He will, as far as practicable, co-operate with Gen. McLaws and Gen. Jackson in intercepting the retreat of the enemy. Gen. D. H. Hill's division will form the rear guard of the army pursuing the road taken by the main body. The reserve artillery, ordnance and supply trains, &c., will precede General Hill.

"General Stuart will detach a squadron of cavalry to accompany the commands of Generals Longstreet, Jackson and McLaws, and, with the main body of the cavalry, will cover the route of the army, and bring up all stragglers that may have been left behind.

"The commands of Generals Jackson, McLaws and Walker, after accomplishing the objects for which they have been detached, will join the main body of the army at Boonsboro or Hagerstown.

"Each regiment on the march will habitually carry its axes in the regimental ordnance. wagons, for use of the men at their encampments to procure wood, &c.

"By Command of GENERAL R. E. LEE,
"R. H. CHILTON, Assistant Adjutant-General,
"MAJ. GEN. D. H. HILL, Commanding Div.

Tablets Erected at Depot at Harper's Ferry, W. Va., by Battlefield Commissioners.

CAPTURE OF HARPER'S FERRY, SUNDAY, 15, 1862.

TABLET I.

On Sept. 10th, 1862, Gen. R. E. Lee, commanding the Army of Northern Virginia, then at Frederick, Md., set three columns in motion to capture Harper's Ferry. Major-Gen. L. McLaws, with his own division and that of Major-Gen. R. H. Anderson, marched through Middletown and Brownsville Pass into Pleasant Valley. On the 12th the brigades of Kershaw and Barksdale ascended Maryland Heights by Solomon's Gap, moved along the crest and at nightfall were checked by the Union forces under command of Col. T. H. Ford, about two miles north of this. Eight Confederate brigades held Weverton, Sandy Hook and approaches from the east. On the 13th Kershaw and Barksdale drove the Union troops from the Heights, Ford, abandoning 7 guns, retreated across the pontoon bridge, a few yards above the railroad bridge to Harper's Ferry. The Union loss was 38 killed and 134 wounded; Confederate loss 35 killed and 178 wounded. Brig.-Gen. John R. Walker's division crossed the Potomac at Point of Rocks, 10 miles below this, during the night of Sept. 10th, and on 13th occupied Loudoun Heights and the roads south of the river, leading east and south.

TABLET II.

Major-Gen. Thomas J. Jackson, with his own division and those of Major-Gen. A. P. Hill and R. S. Ewell, left Frederick on the morning of Sept. 10, and passing through Middletown and Boonsboro, crossed the Potomac at Williamsport, 24 miles north of this, on the afternoon of the 11th. Hill's division took the direct road to Martinsburg and bivouacked near it. Jackson's and Ewell's divisions marched to North Mountain depot on B. & O R. R., seven miles northwest of Martinsburg, and bivouacked. During the night Brigadier-Gen. Julius White, commanding the Union troops at Martinsburg, 2,500 in number, abandoned the place and retreated to Harper's Ferry. Jackson occupied Martinsburg on the morning of the 12th, passed through it and about noon on the 13th, A. P. Hill's division in the advance reached Halltown, 3¼ miles west of this, and went into camp. Jackson and Ewell's divisions, following Hill's, encamped near it.

TABLET III.

Col. Dixon S. Miles, Second U. S. Infantry, commanded the Union forces at Harper's Ferry. After Gen. White joined him from Martinsburg, Sept. 12, and Col. Ford from Maryland Heights on the 13th, Miles had about 14,200 men. On the morning of the 14th the greater part of the force was in position of Bolivar Heights 1½ miles west, its right resting on the Potomac, its left near the Shenandoah, artillery distributed on the line. Artillery and a small force of infantry occupied Camp Hill nearby, midway between this and Bolivar Heights. The cavalry was under partial cover of the irregularities of the ground. On the morning of the 14th, Walker placed five long-range guns near the northern point of Loudoun Heights and at 1 p. m. opened on the Union batteries on Bolivar Heights and Camp Hill, which was replied to. An hour later, Jackson's artillery opened on Bolivar Heights from school house hill and still an hour later McLaws opened from two parrott guns that he had succeeded in placing near the southern extremity of Maryland Heights. The fire from these three directions was continued till silencing and dismounting some of the Union guns.

TABLET IV.

In the afternoon of the 14th Jackson's division advanced its left, seized commanding ground near the Potomac and established artillery upon it. Hill's division moved from Halltown obliquely to the right until it struck the Shenandoah, then pushed along the river. The advance, after some sharp skirmishing, late in the night gained high ground upon which were placed 5 batteries, commanding left rear of the Union line. Ewell's division advanced through Halltown to school house hill and deployed about 1 mile in front of Boliver Heights, bivouacking on either side the Charles Town road. During the night the Confederates advanced on the right and left, gaining some ground and 10 guns of Ewell's division crossed the Shenandoah river at Key's Ford and were placed on the plateau at the foot of Loudoun Heights to enfilade the entire position on Bolivar Heights. About 9 p. m. the entire Union cavalry force, about 1500 men, crossed the pontoon bridge, passed up the canal bank about a mile, followed the mountain road near the river, crossed the Antietam near its mouth, passed through Sharpsburg about midnight and escaped into Pennsylvania.

TABLET V.

At daylight Sept. 15th, the batteries of Jackson's division delivered a severe fire against the right of Bolivar Heights defense. Ewell's batteries opened from School-House hill in front, Hill's five batteries on ground commanding the left of the line and the ten guns across the Shenandoah poured an accurate enfilade fire from the left and rear of Miles' defenses. The artillery on Loudoun Heights and Maryland Heights joined in the attack. This concentrated fire of fifty-six guns was responded to by the Union guns, but in an hour beginning to run short of ammunition. Miles raised the white flag in token of surrender. Soon after he was mortally wounded and the command devolved upon Gen. White who completed the terms of capitulation by the surrender of about 12,000 officers and men and all public property. Hill's division was left to parole the prisoners while Jackson with five divisions marched to the field of Antietam. Exclusive of the loss on Maryland Heights, the Union loss, 9 killed and 39 wounded; Confederate loss, 6 killed and 69 wounded.

The Battles of South Mountain and Antietam, Md.

The battle at Turner's Gap in South Mountain, was fought September 14th, 1862, (Sunday) between Major-General Burnside, commanding right wing of the Union Army, 30,000 to 35,000 strong, and Major-Generals Longstreet and D. H. Hill, of the Confederate Army, 25,000 strong.

The battle at Crampton's Gap, in South Mountain, was fought on the same day as above, between Major-General Franklin's Sixth Corps, forming the left wing of McClellan's Army of the Potomac, 4,000 to 6,000 men, and Brigadier-General Cobb, with two or three brigades of McLaws' division, 1,200 to 1,500 men, while the larger portion of McLaws' division was some miles farther on, operating against Maryland Heights and Harper's Ferry.

The battle of Antietam was fought September 17th, 1862, between the Union Army of the Potomac, 87,000 strong, under Major-General McClellan, and the Confederate Army of Virginia, 97,000 strong, under General R. E. Lee.

The battle of Antietam is tersely and eloquently described in the following address delivered at the unveiling of the soldiers monument September 17, 1880.

ADDRESS OF HON. M. BROSIUS, OF LANCASTER, PA.

This countless assemblage of the children of men declares the profound interest and commanding importance of the occasion that has called us together. Any extraordinary human exertion engages the respectful attention of mankind. A great work of art invokes our admiration, a stupendous effort of intellect commands our reverence. Unexampled feats of daring and prowess affect us with wonder, exhibitions of dauntless courage wrest from us spontaneous applause. But it is the contemplation of a combination of all the elevated powers of man in a state of intense and sublime action —extraordinary physical power of endurance, matchless courage, deathless valor, sublime heroism and noble self-sacrifice, all inspired by a lofty patriotism and a supreme devotion to principles inseparably connected with the maintenance of a just government and the liberties of mankind—that is best fitted to engage all the faculties of the mind—all the emotions of the heart, elevating the whole being to a height from which the sweep of the soul's vision comprehends all that is great in action, admirable in purpose, lofty in sentiment, and god-like in achievement. From such a combination of human endeavors the ground whereon we stand derives its importance in the history of the republic.

To-day, 18 years after its baptism in blood, the name of Antietam is a spear of Aeolus, which smiting the portals of memory, forth rushes a flood of hallowed recollections, on whose uplifting bosom we are borne to a height from which we can survey, with clear and dispassionate vision, the character of that day's supreme test of the mettle of American soldiers, the marvelous results of the sacrifices here piled upon our country's altar, with their great lessons for all coming time.

SOLEMNITY OF THE OCCASION.

How grand the theme, how mighty and far reaching the question its contemplation suggests. Yet how little adapted to the elevated and imposing task of their consideration are the feeble powers of him whom the partiality of the trustee of this beautiful "place of Sepulchers" has chosen for its execution. In the presence of 4,000 of our martyred dead the tongue falters, the heart muffles its beats and a sense of overwhelming awe teaches us that silence rather than words would most accord with the solemnity of the occasion. Whatever we may say of the heroes whose dust repose beneath these mounds, guarded for all time by a nation's imperishable gratitude, symbolized in the sculptured sentinel that stands above them—all our speech will be outweighed by their speechlessness. They are their own best orators to-day, for being dead, they yet speak.

NECESSITY OF THE WAR FOR UNION.

Before alluding to the great event whose commemoration has brought us hither, the solemn inquiry which already subsists in your minds, thrusts itself upon us demanding utterance, "should battles be commemorated in a Christian land." We voice the sentiment of Christendom when we ask, do not all deprecate war? and from this vast multitude bathed in the memory of its inhumanity, its splendid murder, its ghastly horrors, its terrible compensations, comes back, comes back the answer,—"all." Yet to the sense of mankind there is in that answer a reserved exception.

Between the philosophy of Hobbs who held that the natural state of mankind was war, and that super-refined sentiment that there can be no war that is not dishonorable, there is a middle ground whereon the Christian patriot can stand with the assurance of the favor of his country and his God. When the objects of the contest are such as to engage the highest attributes of Heaven and secure alliance between mortal and immortal powers; when necessary to crush bad principles, destroy tyrants and rescue society from evils greater than itself, war becomes a high, noble and responsible duty. When offered by the hand of necessity, not otherwise, said Sir Philip Sidney, it must be accepted. Ours was no rash, fruitless war for wanton glory waged, nor for added power and gain. It was the spontaneous uprising of patriotism to rescue the Union and Liberty. It was precipitated by no ephemeral cause but was in defense of ideas that will wander through eternity—principles inextinguishable as the stars and a civilization which shall endure to the "last vestige of recorded time." It was justified by an over-ruling necessity in the providence of God, in working out the destiny of the nation. It was the shadow by which the sun of American civilization marked its progress on the dial plate of history. It seems to be the lesson of the ages that every new birth of freedom must have its dark night of travail and pain.

THE SEEDS OF CONFLICT.

Liberty and slavery—irreconcilable in their natures—crossed the ocean the same year. The Mayflower and the Dutch slave ship plowed the sea at the same time. Both sought the shores of the new world and both planted their seeds, to grow side by side until the principle of the "*survival of the fittest*" should exterminate the one and nationalize the other. Formidable events in the history of their conflict put thenation to a formidable alternative. The horrors of miasma or the fury of the blast. Said Victor Hugo, for every oak struck with lightning how many forests rendered wholesome. The storm which came behind the visible work was the invisible—the former barbarism—the latter sublime.

Under a scaffolding of war was to be reared a majestic temple of human freedom.

Never before was war so highly justified, for never before had it wrought such achievement for humanity. There were fields on which Spartan valor saved Greek intellect and art from the Persian—fields on which Roman polity and law were saved from the Carthagenians and the Gauls—fields on which Charles Martel hurled back the Saracen hosts from the heart of Christendom—of Marston Moor and Nasby, where at the hands of Fairfax and Cromwell the cavaliers met their doom, of Leipsic, the battle of nations, that delivered Europe from French domination—of Waterloo that saw the overthrow of the first Napoleon and of Sedan that witnessed the downfall of the second empire; but none of these will be so consecrated in after ages as the fields of the American revolution which laid the corner-stone, and of the war for the union which fixed firm and stable forever the foundations of Freedom's empire in the new world.

OBSERVATION TOWER ON BATTLEFIELD.

THE BATTLE.

The silvery vestments of a gray dawn hang upon the hills and drape the woods, along which a desperate and determined foe have formed six miles of double battle lines. In their rear is the Potomac, in front the deep Antietam and McClellan's eager lines. The federal army reaches four miles along the creek. Grim and frowning batteries cover each hill crest, trained upon every stretch of ground over which the soldiers of the Union must pass to scale the steeps oc-

'cupied by the enemy. Death is waiting upon the light of day. It has come. Hooker flings down the gage of battle and advancing beyond the woods, throws his corps like a thunder-bolt against the iron front of Jackson's lines, which fall staggering to the woods beyond. Reinforced by Hood's fresh troops they roll back the blood crested billow sweeping from the field every living thing. Bending before this dreadful storm the lines of Hooker retire. Weakened by his loss, he speeds a message to Doubleday with the command, "give me your best brigade instantly." And it comes, like an avalanche, led by brave Hartsuff—now into the corn field, now against a hurricane of fire against which none but lines of adamant could stand. O ye mortal powers, what courage. How like Gods they move. Yet see how like men they fall—those citizen soldiers who but yesterday left their kisses on the lips of mothers, wives, daughters, in exchange for their benediction as they rushed to the baptism of fire. They came to triumph or to die. See, they still breast that flood of fire; now it begins to break; now, thank God, it is dashed to pieces as a wave upon a rock and ebbs with bloody spray and foam to the sheltered grounds beyond.

The corn-field is again won, but the ground is ridged with the dead.

The gallant Hooker is now borne wounded from the field. But on this there is no gap made in field or staff that is not instantly filled up. Sumner is at hand and bravely he rides into Hooker's place, his white hair streaming in the wind, contrasting with the fiery flash of his eye as he hurries to the thickest of the fight.

But the enemy has rallied again and strengthened by McLaws' and Walker's divisions they advance upon our right, with gleaming bayonets and terrible volleys bend and break our front and hurling it back one-half the distance it had won. But the wave recedes to advance again, for now Franklin comes, his soldiers cheering as they run. They sweep the corn-field again with a tempest of fire which no human power can withstand and on to the woods beyond, from which the shattered lines of the enemy retire, leaving the field which was four times lost and won in the possession of the Union army. It is one o'clock. Burnside wrests the lower bridge from the grasp of the enemy who retreat to the heights. It is three o'clock. Burnside is charging up the steep—the heights are carried—the Confederate right reeling from the shock falls backward almost to Sharpsburg. Glorious triumph. But oh! how short lived.

Another battle line appears, it is Hill's division, and another hurricane of fire leaps from their cannon's mouths. Sorely pressed Burnside sends for help and McClellan replies, "Tell Gen. Burnside this is the battle of the war."

Meanwhile Franklin's batteries are playing on the right like the fires of Ætna. Every hill top is crested with white clouds of smoke. Upon four lines of battle shines that splendid September sun, as it sinks reddening in the west. The night approaches bringing its truce to the dreadful fray. Darkness silences the last gun and the dews of heaven fall upon a crimsoned earth, for

"With copious slaughter all the field was red
And heaped with growing mountains of the dead."

AFTER THE BATTLE.

The battle is over—the field of Antietam has become the valley of the shadow of death. Man is ephemeral; the heavens eternal. The stars that looked down upon that field of blood were the same that lit up the ghostly plains of Troy " rough with the dead bodies of ancient heroes." The moon whose silvery radiance fell upon the up-turned faces of our dead was the same that stood still in the Valley of Ajalon. The marvelous canopy of blue and gold that bent tenderly over that carnival of death was the same that vaulted above the earth at the command of God "Let there be a firmament." The night is past. The first beam of the rising sun kisses the face of 20,000 American soldiers—victors and vanquished. Oh God! what a harvest did the reapers gather that day.

BURNSIDE'S BRIDGE.

"So fought each host with thirst of glory fired,
And crowds on crowds triumphantly expired."

THE FALLEN.

Of those who went down in that holocaust of death what can we say. Vain are the eulogies of the living upon the brave men whom the tide of battle swept to the skies from this historic field. They had the same spirit as Gustavus of Sweden, at Lutzen when he cried "God is my harness." They died in the noblest place for man to die, "at the post of duty; not for themselves but for their country." To their character our praise can add nothing; not to their valor, for it is immortal; not to their patriotism, for it is in the Recording Angel's book; not to their endurance, for it is embalmed in history's page. Helpless to add a single flower to the immortal wreaths that will forever crown their immortal deeds, we resign them to their rest with the prayer of Pennsylvania's sweet poet, on the field of Gettysburg:

> "Take them, O fatherland!
> Who dying, conquered in thy name;
> Take them: O God, our brave
> The glad fulfillment of Thy dread decree,
> Who grasped the sword for peace and smote to save;
> And dying here for freedom, died for Thee."

THE RESULTS OF THE BATTLE.

These were monstrous in extreme. On it was staked the safety of Maryland and Washington, on one side; the deliverance of Maryland and an open highway for Lee to Philadelphia on the other. Had not the rocks of Liberty and Union at Antietam hurled back the waves of rebellion that surged against them the battle of Gettysburg might have been fought in 1862.

Had not the depression that hung like a pall over the north and bowed down the heart of our great president been lifted by this great battle, how the duration of the war might have been affected we cannot tell. But the sun that lit up the field without a foe on the morning of the 18th of September, sent its beams of light and joy into millions of hearts dispelling doubts, allaying fears, inspiring hope. For months a great question had agitated the mind of the president. He felt that the rebellion was vulnerable through slavery; but the public mind was not prepared for it. Fifty thousand bayonets were in the Union army from the border States. Wrestling with this great question day and night he at last declared "whatever shall appear to be God's will I will do." Thus to our noble pilot at the helm, the battle of Antietam was a break in the storm, a gleam of sunlight through a rift in the clouds. He had watched the compass of the popular mind. Two days after the battle, the North, which had been swinging between hope and despair, recovered its courage, and on the wings of praise and thanksgiving millions of hearts went up to God. The hour has come. The nation has been lifted nearer the great source of truth and can now see eye to eye with Him.

Who in the fear of God didst bare the sword of power—a nation's trust and who with prayer upon his lips gives his answer to the invasion of State, by the armies of the rebellion. That proclamation "*time's noblest act*" received the approval of men and the gracious favor of God; and the war for the first time assumed its real character. At the close of the battle of Valmy, Gothe said, "From this time and from this place commences a new era in the world's history and you can all say you were present at its birth." From this place and from the day we commemorate is a new era in American history and thousands of American soldiers can say "we were present at its birth." When the struggle for the Union was thus elevated, when men saw that the hopes of humanity hung upon a battle, it seemed that the heavens became more propitious, until joyful peace extinguished the camp fires on the last battlefield and the republic marched with stately tread over the elevated plain which had become the theater of the grandest drama in human history, whose acts followed by inevitable logic until the nation borrowed the mighty words of Sinai's burning mount : "Proclaim liberty throughout all the land, unto all the inhabitants thereof;" sublime consummation. The whole earth felt the instantaneous thrill as the sun of freedom burst in full-orbed splendor upon the new world, sending beams parallel with the eternal law into the remotest refuge of oppression.

"For mankind are one in spirit and an instinct beats along
Round the earth's electric circle the swift flash of right and wrong,
Whether conscious or unconscious, yet humanities vast frame
Through its ocean sundered fibers feels the gush of joy or shame.
In the gain or loss of one race, all the rest have an equal claim."

Crowned thus with the artist's last band the column of American liberty stands surmounted with the presiding genius of the work, with outstretched hands invoking and receiving the blessings of God. Thus is exhibited the effects of the battle of Antietam—a rich heritage of glory whose lustre is as fadeless and whose life is as perennial as the stars.

THE VEIL LIFTED.

At last the veil was lifted and displayed an exalted mission and splendid destiny for the republic. As you silent sentinel (pointing to the statue) watches the honored dead, so we will guard the priceless legacies left us. Oh! my countrymen, do we realize the task imposed upon us. Are we fit for the exalted service? This question is propounded, by the field of Antietam, to the nation today. If the patriotism of all sections answers yea, then the American republic shall stand a monument to its patriot dead when pyramids are not and the Karnak is forgotten.

OUR COUNTRY.

What is our country that we should be thus mindful of it? 13 Colonies have grown into 38 Commonwealths. The 3,000,000 have multiplied into 50,000,000, obeying one law, having one country. Our commerce whitens every sea; railroads span the continent; the telegraph makes every community the centre of the worlds chronicles. Our science and invention augment man's power. Here the very child can be educated. At the recent exhibition of various and multiplied industries, we competed with the world and our products were peerless. The clustered trophies of the world's conquest in science and art, manufactures and agriculture were side by side in friendly rivalship, on our own soil and amidst them all the young Republic of America rose in queenly majesty and stood proudly eminent.

DUNKARD'S CHURCH, ON HAGERSTOWN PIKE.

MORAL GREATNESS AND MAGNANIMITY.

Those deeds of kindness performed with equal tenderness, whether to relieve the wracking pain of mutilated soldier in blue or to cool the fevered brow of one clad in gray, were pinions on which many loyal souls, North and South, rose as on bright wings toward Heaven. Thus above all questions of time and sense, above the Union, above rebellion, was the boundless compassion of the human soul illuminating with the light of divine actions the dark precipice of civil strife.

And when the greatest living soldier laid his conquering sword on the capital of the Confederacy and received the surrender of Gen. Lee, and when the curtain fell before the tragedy of the rebellion, voicing the sentiment of the North, he said, "Lay down your arms and go to your homes on the parole of honor," and the nation said "Go and sin no more." The great Cæsar wrote to a friend that the chief enjoyment he had of his victory, was of seeing every day one or other of his fellow citizens who had borne arms against him.

LESSONS OF THE BATTLE.

The great lesson is that we strive for a standard of moral independence, political integrity, obedience and loyalty which will guarantee a citizenship at once independent, incorruptible, obedient to law and loyal to the public weal. Without a vigorous, noble and true manhood, though our empire reach from sea to sea, we are a rope of sand.

"Ill fares the land, to hastening ills a prey
Where wealth accumulates and men decay."

RECONCILIATION.

Reconciliation and forgiveness are as important now as were heroism and valor in the hour of our country's peril. If there remains upon the Union a single strain of sectional hate let us not rest until it is wiped away. After the surrender Gen. Lee made the great speech of his life; he said, "soldiers we have done our duty and we know it; now let us go home and be good citizens." The nation's silent chieftains also said, "Let us have peace." The prayer we utter from Antietam to-day is, "Let us have peace." Let us be good citizens. From the hearts of patriots everywhere, attuned to the same melody, is lifted up the glad refrain—celestial choirs prolong the joyful chorus, until the spirits of our martyred dead send back the swelling anthem, "Let us have peace; let us be good citizens."

Thus may a true unity of patriotic faith be restored in all hearts that are *now* loyal, and the people North and South rising above the mists of earth—the smoke of battle—the clouds of resentment and hate into the golden sunlight of their better natures, will find their rock of reconciliation in the reflection that the dark and stormy path of war was the way of light to a redeemed and regenerated republic.

HOPES OF THE FUTURE.

Having indulged some reflections which emanated from this occasion; having witnessed this solemn "guard mounting" over the dead; having dedicated this colossal soldier to his high task and been ourselves dedicated to a yet higher and holier one, may we not, without invoking the necromancer or astrologer, without searching among the silent stars, but from a consideration of the past and present alone, predict for the future of our country a career far transcending in the grandeur of its achievements anything the world has yet attained,

"That cast in some diviner mould
The new cycle shall shame the old."

Animated by these views and inspired by these hopes, Americans can hold fast their faith, that while this granite sentinel shall hold his silent watch above these graves, yea, when the battle of time shall have cut him down also, and his dust shall have mingled with that of the dead beneath him, the Republic, guided by principles that follow in the wake of Christianity as verdure follows the sun, freighted with golden triumphs of the past and led by faith in an immortal destiny, "as by a pillar of cloud by day and of fire by night," will continue her majestic march down the centuries, plucking new laurels and winning new victories for man and government, until, ripe with years and a completed destiny, she lays the finished crown of her glory at the feet of Jehovah at the jubilee of eternity.

BLOODY LANE, EAST OF HAGERSTOWN PIKE.

Official Reports of Major-General Geo. B. McClellan of the Battles of South Mountain and Antietam.

HEADQUARTERS, NEAR SHARPSBURG, MD.,
Sept. 29, 1862.

I have the honor to report the following as some of the results of the battles of South Mountain and Antietam: At South Mountain our loss was 443 killed, 1,806 wounded, and 76 missing; total, 2,325. At Antietam our loss was 2,010 killed, 9,416 wounded, and 1,043 missing; total, 12,469. Total loss in the two battles, 14,794, (but see revised statement of casualties.) The loss of the rebels in the two battles, as near as can be ascertained from the number of their dead found upon the field, and from other data, will not fall short of the following estimate: Major Davis, assistant inspector-general, who superintends the burial of the dead, reports about 3,000 rebels buried upon the field of Antietam by our own troops. Previous to this, however, the rebels had buried many of their own dead upon the distant portion of the battlefield, which they occupied after the battle—probably at least 500. The loss of the rebels at South Mountain cannot be ascertained with accuracy; but as our troops continually drove them from the commencement of the action, and a much greater number of their dead were seen on the field than our own men, it is not unreasonable to suppose that their loss was greater than ours. Estimating their killed at 500, the total rebel killed in the two battles would be 4,000, according to the ratio of our own killed and wounded. This would make their loss in wounded 18,742, as nearly as can be determined at this time. The number of prisoners taken by our troops in the two battles will, at the lowest estimate, amount to 5,000. The full returns will no doubt show a larger number. Of these about 1,200 are wounded. This gives the rebel loss in killed and wounded and prisoners 25,542. It will be observed that this does not include their stragglers, the number of whom is said by citizens here to be large. It may be safely concluded, therefore, that the Rebel army lost 30,000 of their best troops during their brief campaign in Maryland. From the time our troops first encountered the enemy in Maryland, until he was driven back into Virginia, we captured 13 guns, 7 caissons, 9 limbers, 2 field forges, 2 caisson bodies, 39 colors, and 1 signal flag. We have not lost a single gun or color on the battlefield of Antietam. Fourteen thousand small arms were collected, besides the large number carried off by citizens and those distributed on the ground to recruits and other unarmed men arriving immediately after the battle. At South Mountain no collection of small arms was made, owing to the haste of the pursuit from that point. Four hundred were taken on the opposite side of the Potomac.

GEO. B. McCLELLAN,
Major-General Commanding.

MAJOR-GEN. HALLECK, General-in-chief.

General Orders, No. 160.

HEADQUARTERS ARMY OF THE POTOMAC,
CAMP NEAR SHARPSBURG, MD., Oct. 3rd, 1862.

The commanding general extends his congratulations to the army under his command for the victories achieved by their bravery at the passes of the South Mountain and upon the Antietam Creek. The brilliant conduct of Reno's and Hooker's corps under Burnside, at Turner's Gap, and of Franklin's corps at Crampton's Pass, in which, in the face of an enemy strong in position and resisting with obstinacy, they carried the mountain and prepared the way for the advance of the army, won for them the admiration of their brethren in arms.

In the memorable battle of Antietam we defeated a numerous and powerful army of the enemy, in an action desperately fought and remarkable for its duration and for the destruction of life which attended it. The obstinate bravery of the troops of Hooker, Mansfield and Sumner, the dashing gallantry of those of Franklin on the right, the sturdy valor of those of Burnside on the left, and the vigorous support of Porter and Pleasanton, present a brilliant spectacle to our countrymen which will swell their hearts with pride and exultation. Fourteen guns, 39 colors, 15,500 stands of arms, and nearly 6,000 prisoners taken from the enemy, are evidences of the completeness of our triumph. A grateful country will thank this noble army for achievements which have rescued the loyal States of the East from the ravages of the invader and have driven him from their borders.

While rejoicing at the victories which, under God's blessing, have crowned our exertions, let us cherish the memory of our brave companions who have laid down their lives upon the battlefield, martyrs in their country's cause, their names will ever be enshrined in the hearts of the people.

By command of
Major-General McCLELLAN.

S. WILLIAMS, Assistant Adjutant-General.

General Lee, in his official report to President Davis, says of these battles:

SHARPSBURG, MD., Sept. 16th, 1862.

MR. PRESIDENT: My letter to you of the 13th instant informed you of the positions of the different divisions of this army. Learning that night that Harper's Ferry had not surrendered, and that the enemy was advancing more rapidly than was convenient from Fredericktown, I determined to return with Longstreet's command to the Blue Ridge, to strengthen D. H. Hill's and Stuart's divisions, engaged in holding the passes of the mountains, lest the enemy should fall upon McLaws' rear, drive him from the Maryland Heights, and thus relieve the garrison at Harper's Ferry. On approaching Boonsboro, I received information from General D. H. Hill that the enemy in strong force was at the main pass on the Frederick and Hagerstown road, pressing him so heavily as to require immediate re-inforcements. Longstreet advanced rapidly to his support and immediately placed his troops in position. By this time Hill's right had been forced back, the gallant Garland having fallen in rallying his brigade. Under Gen. Longstreet's directions, our right was soon restored and firmly resisted the attacks of the enemy to the last. His superior numbers enabled him to extend beyond both of our flanks, and his right was able to reach the summit of the mountain to our left and press us heavily in that direction. The battle raged until after night. The enemy's efforts to force a passage were resisted, but we had been unable to repulse him. Learning later in the evening that Crampton's Gap, (on the direct road from Fredericktown to Sharpsburg,) had been forced, and McLaws' rear thus threatened, and believing from a report from Gen. Jackson that Harper's Ferry would fall next morning, I determined to withdraw Longstreet and D. H. Hill from their positions and retire to the vicinity of Sharpsburg, where the army could be more easily united. Before abandoning the position, indications led me to believe that the enemy was withdrawing, but learning from a prisoner that Sumner's corps, (which had not been engaged,) was being put in position to relieve their wearied troops, while the most of ours were exhausted by a fatiguing march and a hard conflict, and I feared would be unable to renew the fight successfully in the morning, confirmed me in my determination. Accordingly, the troops were withdrawn, preceded by the trains, without molestation by the enemy, and about daybreak took position in front of this place. The enemy did not pass through the gap until about 8 o'clock of the morning after the battle, and their advance reached a position in front of us about 2 p. m. Before their arrival, I received intelligence from Gen. Jackson that Harper's Ferry had surrendered early in the morning. From a more detailed statement furnished by Gen. Jackson's Adjutant-General, it appears that 49 pieces of artillery, 24 mountain howitzers and 17 revolving guns, 11,000 men fit for duty (consisting of twelve regiments of infantry, three companies of cavalry, and six companies of artillery,) together with 11,000 small arms, were the fruits of this victory.

Part of Gen. Jackson's corps has reached us and the rest are approaching, except Gen. A. P. Hill's division, left at Harper's Ferry to guard the place and take care of public property. The enemy have made no attack up to this afternoon, but are in force in our front. This victory of the indomitable Jackson and his troops gives us renewed occasion for gratitude to Almighty God for His guidance and protection.

I am, with high respect, your obedient servant,

R. E. LEE, General.

His Excellency, PRESIDENT DAVIS.

HEADQUARTERS, SHARPSBURG, MD., Sept. 18th, 1862.

MR. PRESIDENT: On the afternoon of the 16th instant the enemy, who, you were informed on that day, was in our front, opened a light fire of artillery upon our line. Early next morning it was renewed in earnest, and large masses of the Federal troops that had crossed the Antietam above our position assembled on our left and threatened to overwhelm us. They advanced in three compact lines. The divisions of Generals McLaws, R. H. Anderson, A. P. Hill and Walker had not arrived the previous night, as I had hoped, and were still beyond the Potomac. Generals Jackson's and Ewell's divisions were thrown to the left of Generals D. H. Hill and Longstreet. The enemy advanced between the Antietam and Sharpsburg and Hagerstown turnpike, and was met by Gen. Hill's and the left of Gen. Longstreet's division, where the contest raged fiercely, extending to our entire left. The enemy was driven back and held in check, but before the divisions of McLaws, Anderson and Walker, who upon their arrival on the morning of the 17th were advanced to support the left wing and center, could be brought into action, that portion of our lines was forced back by superior numbers. The line, after a severe conflict, was restored and the enemy driven back, and our position maintained during the rest of the day. In the afternoon the enemy advanced on our right, where Gen. Jones' division was posted, who handsomely maintained his position. Gen. Toombs' brigade, guarding the bridge over Antietam Creek, (known as Burnside Bridge) gallantly resisted the approach of the enemy; but his superior numbers enabling him to extend his left, he crossed below the bridge, and assumed a threatening attitude on our right, which fell back in confusion. By this time, between 3 and 4 P. M., Gen. A. P. Hill, with five of his brigades, reached the scene of action, drove the enemy immediately from the position they had taken, and continued the contest until dark, restoring our right and maintaining our ground.

        R. E. LEE, General Commanding.

His Excellency, PRESIDENT DAVIS, Richmond, Va.

    HEADQUARTERS ARMY OF NORTHERN VIRGINIA,
        September 20th, 1862.

SIR: Since my last letter to you of the 18th, finding the enemy indisposed to make an attack on that day, and our position being a bad one to hold with the river in rear, I determined to cross the army to the Virginia side. This was done at night successfully, nothing being left behind, unless it may have been some disabled guns or broken-down wagons, and the morning of the 19th found us satisfactorily over on the south bank of the Potomac, near Shepherdstown, when the army was immediately put in motion toward Williamsport. Before crossing the river, in order to threaten the enemy on his right and rear and make him apprehensive for his communications, I sent the cavalry forward to Williamsport, which they successfully occupied. At night the infantry sharp-shooters left, in conjunction with General Pendleton's Artillery, to hold the ford below Shepherdstown, gave back, and the enemy's cavalry took possession of that town, and from General Pendleton's report after midnight, I fear much of his reserve artillery has been captured. I am now obliged to return to Shepherdstown, with the intention of driving the enemy back, if not in position with his whole army; but. if in full force, I think an attack would be inadvisable, and I shall make other dispositions.

   I am, with high respect, your obedient servant,
        R. E. LEE, General.

His excellency, JEFFERSON DAVIS, Richmond, Va.

ORGANIZATION OF THE ARMY OF THE POTOMAC.

MAJOR-GENERAL GEO. B. MCCLELLAN, U. S. ARMY, COMMANDING, SEPT. 14 TO 17, 1862.

GENERAL HEADQUARTERS.
ESCORT.
Capt. James B. McIntyre.

Independent Company, Oneida, (New York) Cavalry, Capt. Daniel P. Mann.
4th U. S. Cavalry, Company A, Lieut. Thomas H. McCormick.
4th U. S. Cavalry, Company E, Capt. Jas. B. McIntyre.

VOLUNTEER ENGINEER BRIGADE,
Brig.-Gen. Daniel P. Woodberry.

15th New York, Col. John McL. Murphy.
50th New York, Lieut.-Col. William H. Pettes.

REGULAR ENGINEER BATTALION,
Capt. James C. Duane.

PROVOST GUARD,
Major William H. Wood.

2nd U. S. Cavalry, Companies E, F, H and K, Capt. Geo. A. Gordon.
8th U. S. Infantry, Companies A, D, F and G, Capt. Royal T. Frank.
19th U. S. Infantry, Company G, Capt. Edmund L. Smith.
19th U. S. Infantry, Company H, Capt. Henry S. Welton.

HEADQUARTERS' GUARD.
Major Granville O. Haller.

Sturge's (Illinois) Rifles, Capt. James Steel.
93rd New York, Lieut.-Col. Benjamin C. Butler.

QUARTERMASTER'S GUARD.

1st U. S. Cavalry, Companies B, C and I, Capt. Marcus A. Reno.

FIRST ARMY CORPS:
1. Maj.-Gen. Joseph Hooker. (Wounded Sept. 17th.)
2. Brig.-Gen. George A. Meade.

ESCORT.

2nd New York Cavalry, Companies A, B, I and K, Capt. John E. Naylor.

FIRST DIVISION.

Brig.-Gen. Abner Doubleday.

SECOND DIVISION.
Brig.-Gen. James B. Ricket.
THIRD DIVISION.
1. Brig.-Gen. George G. Meade, (1st Corps.)
2. Brig.-Gen. Truman Seymour.

SECOND CORPS.
Maj.-Gen. Edwin V. Sumner.

ESCORT.
6th New York Cavalry, Company D, Capt. Henry W. Lyon.
6th New York Cavalry, Company K. Capt. Riley Johnson.

FIRST DIVISION.
1. Maj.-Gen. Israel B. Richardson, (Wounded September 17th.)
2. Brig.-Gen. John C. Caldwell, 1st Brigade.
3. Brig.-Gen. Winfield S. Hancock.
1st, 2nd and 3rd Brigades, consisting of 14 Regiments Infantry, 2 Batteries Artillery.

SECOND DIVISION.
1. Major-Gen. John Sedgwick, (Wounded September 17th.)
2. Brig.-Gen. Oliver O. Howard.
1st, 2nd and 3rd Brigades, consisting of 13 Regiments Infantry, 2 Companies Sharp-shooters, 2 Batteries Artillery.

THIRD DIVISION.
Brig.-Gen. William H. French.
1st, 2nd and 3rd Brigades, consisting of 10 Regiments Infantry, 3 Batteries Artillery.

FOURTH ARMY CORPS.
FIRST DIVISION,
Maj.-Gen. Darius N. Couch.
1st, 2nd and 3rd Brigades, consisting of 15 Regiments Infantry, 4 Batteries Artillery, assigned to 6th Corps, as the 3rd Division, September 26, 1862.

FIFTH ARMY CORPS.
Maj.-Gen. Fitz John Porter.
ESCORT.
1st Maine Cavalry, detachment, Capt. Geo. J. Summat.
FIRST DIVISION,
Maj.-Gen. Geo. W. Morrell.
1st, 2nd and 3rd Brigades, consisting of 19 Regiments Infantry,

ANTIETAM.

3 Companies Sharp-shooters, 3 Batteries Artillery.

SECOND DIVISION,
Brig.-Gen. George Sykes.

1st, 2nd and 3rd Brigades, consisting of 10 United States Battalions Infantry, 2 Regiments Infantry, 3 Batteries Artillery.

THIRD DIVISION,
Brig.-Gen. Andrew A. Humphreys.

1st and 2nd Brigades, consisting of 8 Pennsylvania Regiments Infantry, 2 Batteries Artillery. (This Division was organized September 12th, and reached the battlefield September 18th.)

ARTILLERY RESERVE,
Lieut.-Col. William Hays.

5 Battalions New York Light Batteries, 2 United States Batteries.

SIXTH ARMY CORPS:
Maj.-William B. Franklin.

ESCORT,

6th Pennsylvania Cavalry. Companies B and G, Capt. Henry P. Muirheid.

FIRST DIVISION,
Maj.-Gen. Henry W. Slocum.

1st, 2nd and 3rd Brigades, consisting of 12 Regiments Infantry. 4 Batteries Artillery.

SECOND DIVISION,
Maj.-Gen. William F. Smith.

1st, 2nd and 3rd Brigades, consisting of 15 Regiments Infantry, 3 Batteries Artillery.

NINTH ARMY CORPS:

1. Maj.-Gen. Ambrose E. Burnside. (commanding left wing.)
2. Maj.-Gen. Jesse L. Reno. (killed September 14th.)
3. Brig.-Gen. Jacob D. Cox.

ESCORT.

1st Maine Cavalry. Company G, Capt. Zebulon B. Blethen.

FIRST DIVISION.
Brig.-Gen. Orlando B. Willcox.

1st and 2nd Brigades, consisting of 8 Regiments Infantry, 2 Batteries Artillery.

SECOND DIVISION,

BRIG.-GEN. SAMUEL D. STURGIS.

1st and 2nd Brigades, consisting of 8 Regiments Infantry, 2 Batteries Artillery.

THIRD DIVISION,

BRIG.-GEN. ISAAC P. RODMAN, (wounded September 17th.)

1st and 2nd Brigades, consisting of 7 Regiments Infantry, 1 Battery (5th U. S.) Artillery.

KANAWHA DIVISION,

1. Brig.-Gen Jacob D. Cox.
2. Col. Eliakim P. Scammon.

1st and 2nd Brigades, consisting of 6 Regiments Infantry, 4 Companies Cavalry, 3 Batteries Artillery.

TWELFTH ARMY CORPS:

1. Maj.-Gen. Joseph K. F. Mansfield, (killed September 17th.)
2. Brig.-Gen. Alpheus S. Williams.

ESCORT,

1st Michigan Cavalry, Company L, Capt. Melvin Brewer.

FIRST DIVISION,

1. Brig.-Gen. Alpheus S. Williams.
2. Brig.-Gen. Samuel W. Crawford, (wounded September 17th.)
3. Brig.-Gen. Geo. H. Gordon.

1st and 2nd Brigades, consisting of 10 Regiments Infantry.

SECOND DIVISION,

BRIG.-GEN. GEO. S. GREENE.

1st, 2nd and 3rd Brigades, consisting of 13 Regiments Infantry, 7 Batteries Artillery.

CAVALRY DIVISION,

BRIG.-GEN. ALFRED PLEASANTON.

1st, 2nd, 3rd, 4th and 5th Brigades, consisting of 14 Battalions Cavalry, 4 Batteries Artillery.

ORGANIZATION OF THE ARMY OF NORTHERN VA.,
GENERAL ROBERT E. LEE, COMMANDING DURING THE MARYLAND CAMPAIGN.

LONGSTREET'S CORPS:
MAJOR-GENERAL JAMES LONGSTREET.

Major-General Lafayette McLaws' Division, consisting,
Kershaw's Brigade, 4 Regiments.
Semmes'   "   4   "
Coffs'   "   4   "
Barksdale's "   4   "
Major S. P. Hamilton, } Commanding 5 Batteries Artillery.
Captain H. C. Cabell, }

Major-General Richard H. Anderson's Division, consisting,
Wilcox's Brigade, 4 Regiments.
Armstead's   "   5   "
Mahone's   "   5   "
Pryor's   "   4   "
Featherstone's " 4   "
Wright's   "   4   "
Major John S. Saunders, Commanding 4 Batteries Artillery.

Brigadier-General David R. Jones' Division, consisting,
Toombs' Brigade, 4 Regiments.
Drayton's   "   3   "
Pickett's   "   5   "
Jenkins'   "   5   "
Anderson's   "   5   "
Four Batteries Artillery, (Virginia.)

Brigadier-General John G. Walker's Division, consisting,
Walker's Brigade, 5 Regiments and 1 Battery.
Ransom's   "   4   "   "   1   "

Brigadier-General John B. Hood's Division, consisting,
Hood's Brigade, 4 Regiments.
Laws'   "   4   "
Evans'   "   5   "
Major B. W. Trobel, Commanding 3 Batteries Artillery.
Colonel J. B. Walton's, Washington, (Louisiana,) 4 Companies Artillery.
Colonel S. D. Lee's Battalion, 6 Batteries Artillery.

JACKSON'S CORPS:

MAJOR-GENERAL THOMAS J. JACKSON.

Major-General Ewell's Division, consisting,
    Lawton's Brigade, 6 Regiments.
    Trumble's   "   5   "
    Early's   "   7   "
    Hays'   "   5   "
    Major A. R. Courtney, Commanding, 7 Batteries Artillery.

Major-General Ambrose P. Hill's Light Division,
    Branche's Brigade, 5 Regiments.
    Archer's   "   5   "
    Gregg's   "   5   "
    Pender's   "   4   "
    Field's   "   4   "
    Thomas'   "   4   "
    Major R. L. Walker, Commanding, 7 Batteries Artillery.

Major-General Jackson's Division, consisting,
    Winder's Brigade, 5 Regiments.
    Jones'   "   4   "
    Taliaferro's "   5   "
    Starke's   "   6   "
    Major L. M. Shoemaker, Commanding, 6 Batteries Artillery.

Major-General David H. Hill's Division, consisting,
    Ripley's Brigade, 4 Regiments.
    Garland's "   5   "
    Rode's   "   5   "
    Anderson's "   4   "
    Colquitt's "   5   "
    Major Pierson, Commanding, 4 Batteries Artillery.

Brigadier-General William N. Pendleton, (chief command) Reserve Artillery.
    Brown's Battalion, 5 Batteries.
    Jones'   "   4   "
    Cutt's   "   5   "
    Nelson's   "   5   "

MISCELLANEOUS:

Five Batteries Virginia Artillery.
Major-General James E. B. Stewart, Cavalry, consisting,
    Hampton's Brigade, 5 Regiments.
    Lee's   "   5   "
    Robertson's "   5   "
    Capt. John Pelham, Commanding, 3 Batteries Horse Artillery.

ANTIETAM.

Return of Casualties in the Union Forces in the Battle of Antietam on the 16th and 17 of Sept., 1862.	Killed Officers	Killed Enlisted Men	Wounded Officers	Wounded Enlisted Men	Captured or Missing Officers	Captured or Missing Enlisted Men	Aggregate
First Corps. Maj.-Gen. Joseph Hooker, (Sept. 17.) Brig.-Gen. Geo. G. Meade.			1				1
First Division, Brig.-Gen. Abner Doubleday.	10	130	34	604		34	812
Second Division, Brig.-Gen. James B. Rickets.	6	166	43	903		86	1204
Third Division, 1. Brig.-Gen. George G. Meade,(1 C'ps) 2. Brig.-Gen. Truman Seymour.	9	96	22	444		2	573
Total, First Army Corps,	25	392	100	1951		122	2590
Second Corps. Major-Gen. Edwin V. Sumner. Staff.			2				2
First Division, 1. Maj.-Gen. Israel B. Richardson, (17.) 2. Brig.-Gen. John C. Caldwell. 3. Brig.-Gen. Winfield S. Hancock.	19	191	46 1	893	16	1165 1
Second Division. 1. Maj.-Gen. John Sedgwick, (17.) 2. Brig.-Gen. Oliver O. Howard.	23	350	80 1	1513	3	241	2210
Third Division, Brig.-Gen. William H. French.	21	278	60	1255		136	1750
Unattached Artillery,		1		9			10
Total, Second Army Corps,	63	820	188	3671	3	393	5138
Fourth Corps—First Division, Maj.-Gen. Darius N. Couch. (Not engaged in the battle proper.) *Fifth Corps,* Maj.-Gen. Fitz John Porter. (only a portion of the Corps engaged.)			1	8			9
Second Division, Brig.-Gen. Geo. Sykes.		12	2	83		1	98
Artillery Reserve, Lieut.-Col. William Hays.	1	4		5		1	11
Total Fifth Army Corps.	1	16	2	88		2	109
Sixth Corps, Maj.-Gen. William B. Franklin. Staff.	1						
First Division, Maj.-Gen. Henry W. Slocum.		5	2	56		2	65
Second Division, Maj.-Gen. William F. Smith,	7	58	20	257	2	29	473
Total, Sixth Army Corps,	8	63	22	313	2	31	439

Casualties in the Union Forces, &c., continued. Major-Gen. Burnside commanding left wing.	Killed		Wounded		Captured or Missing		
	Officers	Enlisted Men	Officers	Enlisted Men	Officers	Enlisted Men	Aggregate
Ninth Corps, Brig.-Gen. Jacob D. Cox.							
First Division, Brig.-Gen. Orlando B. Willcox.	2	44	20	265		7	338
Second Division, Brig.-Gen. Samuel D. Sturgis.	9	127	33	499		11	679
Third Division, Brig.-Gen. Isaac P. Rodman.	8	212	41	746	1	70	1077
Kanawha Division, Col. Eliakim B. Scammon.	5	31	4	188	2	25	255
Total, Ninth Army Corps,	24	414	99	1698	2	113	2349
Twelfth Corps, 1. Maj.-Gen. Joseph K. F. Mansfield. 2. Brig.-Gen. Alpheus S. Williams.	1						
First Division, 1. Brig.-Gen. Alpheus S. Williams. 2. Brig.-Gen. Samuel W. Crawford. 3. Brig.-Gen. Geo. H. Gordon.	9	150	37 1	827		54	1077
Second Division. Brig.-Gen. Geo. S. Greene.	7	107	26	481		30	651
Artillery, Capt. Clermont L. Best.		1		15		1	17
Total, Twelfth Army Corps,	17	258	63	1323		85	1746
Cavalry Division, Brig.-Gen. Alfred Pleasanton.	1	6		23			30
RECAPITULATION.							
First Army Corps,	25	392	100	1951		122	2590
Second Army Corps,	63	820	188	3671	3	393	5138
Fourth Army Corps, (First Division,)			1	8			9
Fifth Army Corps,	1	16	2	88		2	109
Sixth Army Corps,	8	63	22	313	2		439
Ninth Army Corps,	24	414	98	1698	2	31	2349
Twelfth Army Corps,	17	258	63	1323		113	1746
Cavalry Division,	1	6		23		85	30
Total, Army of the Potomac,	139	1969	474	9075	7	746	12410

ANTIETAM.

Casualties in the Union forces in the battles, Turner's Gap and Crampton's Gap, in South Mountain, Sept. 14th, 1862. Major-General A. E. Burnside commanding right wing, Army of the Potomac.

	Killed		Wounded		Captured or Missing		Aggregate
	Officers	Enlisted Men	Officers	Enlisted Men	Officers	Enlisted Men	
First Army Corps, Maj.-Gen. Joseph Hooker.							
First Division, 1. Brig.-Gen. John P. Hatch. 2. Brig.-Gen. Abner Doubleday.	1	62	14 1	375	43		496
Second Division, Brig.-Gen. James B. Rickett.		9	2	24			35
Third Division, Brig.-Gen. Geo. G. Meade.	7	88	16	280	1		392
Sixth Army Corps, Maj.-Gen. William B. Franklin.							
First Division, Maj.-Gen. Henry W. Slocum.	5	107	18	381	2		513
Second Division, Maj.-Gen. William F. Smith.		1	1	18			20
Ninth Army Corps, 1. Maj.-Gen. Jesse L. Reno. 2. Brig.-Gen. Jacob D. Cox.	1						
First Division, Brig.-Gen. Orlando B. Willcox.	2	62	13	278			355
Second Division, Brig.-Gen. Samuel D. Sturgis.	1	9	5	112	30		157
Third Division, Brig.-Gen. Isaac P. Rodman.		2	1	17			20
Kanawha Division, 1. Brig.-Gen. Jacob D. Cox.	1	79	14	251	11		356
Cavalry Division, (Pleasanton.)			1				1
Grand Total,	18	420	85	1736	87		2346

MARKING THE LINES OF BATTLE AND THE POSITIONS OF TROOPS OF THE ARMY OF THE POTOMAC AND THE ARMY OF NORTHERN VIRGINIA AT ANTIETAM, MARYLAND, ETC.

FEBRUARY 27, 1891.—Committed to the Committee of the whole House on the state of the Union and ordered to be printed.

MR. LANSING, from the Committee on Military Affairs, submitted the following report:

The purpose is to have each State which had troops engaged on the field provide the monuments for marking the positions of the troops, after the general plan heretofore pursued at Gettysburg by the Gettysburg Battlefield Memorial Association, and proposed by the Chickamauga Memorial Association for like purposes on the fields of Chickamauga and Chattanooga. The sole expense to the United States for monuments will be those for marking the positions of the regular regiments and batteries, being 42.

The regular Army had 16 regiments and 26 batteries on this field, which the District of Columbia and the following nineteen States had troops in the Union Army: Maine, Massachusetts, New Hampshire, Vermont, Rhode Island, Connecticut, New York, New Jersey, Pennsylvania, Delaware, Maryland, Ohio, West Virginia, Indiana, Kentucky, Illinois, Michigan, Wisconsin and Minnesota. The Confederate Army was represented by troops from Virginia, North Carolina, South Carolina, Georgia, Florida, Alabama, Mississippi, Tennessee, Louisiana, Arkansas, and Texas. On no other field was the Regular Army so largely represented, on no other field was there such a full representation of States, and nowhere did they have representatives that excelled the desperate fighting done on that field.

As already stated, Antietam was the bloodiest battle of the war of the rebellion. More men were killed on that one day than on any other one day of the war. There were battles with greater loss of life, but they were not fought out in one day as at Antietam. At Gettysburg, Chancellorsville, and Spottsylvania, the fighting covered 3 days or more; at the Wilderness, Cold Harbor, Shiloh, Stone River, Chickamauga and Atlanta, the losses were divided between two days of fighting; but at Antietam the bloody work commenced at sunrise and by 4 o'clock that afternoon it was over. A table showing the losses in the

ANTIETAM. 89

principal engagements of the war presents these facts more definitely.

	Date.	Killed.	Wounded.	Missing	Aggregate.
Antietam	Sept. 17, 1862	2,108	9,549	753	12,410
Gettysburg	July 1-3, 1863	3,070	14,497	5,434	23,001
Spottsylvania	May 8-18, 1864	2,725	13,416	2,258	18,393
Wilderness	May 5-7, 1864	2,246	12,037	3,383	17,666
Chancellorsville	May 1-3, 1863	1,606	9,762	5,919	17,287
Chickamauga	Sept. 19-20, 1863	1,656	9,749	4,774	16,179
Cold Harbor	June 1-4, 1864	1,844	9,077	1,816	12,737
Fredericksburgh	Dec. 11-14, 1863	1,284	9,600	1,769	12,653
Manassas	Aug. 28-30, 1862	1,747	8,452	4,263	14,462
Shiloh	April 6-7, 1862	1,754	8,408	2,885	13,047
Stone River	Dec. 31, 1862; Jan. 12, 1863.	1,730	7,802	3,717	13,249
Petersburgh	June 15-19, 1864	1,688	8,513	1,185	11,386
Atlanta, including Peach Tree and Ezra Church and battle of July 22.	July 1-31, 1864	1,110	5,915	2,694	9,719
Chattanooga	Nov. 23-25, 1863	687	4,346	349	5,382

The percentage of loss on the Union side was over 15 per cent. of the entire strength of the Army and fully 20 per cent. of the troops under fire. Many brigades lost one-third to one-half the men taken into action, and twelve regiments lost more than 50 per cent., the Twelfth Massachutts heading the list with 67 per cent., while the lowest of the twelve, the Fourteenth Indiana, lost 56 per cent.

Wellington lost 12 per cent. at Waterloo; Napoleon 14½ per cent. at Austerlitz and 14 per cent. at Marengo. The average losses of both armies at Magenta and Solferino, in 1859, was less than 9 per cent. At Koniggratz, in 1866, it was 6 per cent. At Worth, Mars-la-Tour, Gravelotte, and Sedan, in 1870, the average loss was 12 per cent.

The marvel of German fighting in the Franco-Prussian was by the Third Westphalian Infantry at Mars-la-Tour. It took 3,000 men into action and lost 40.4 per cent. Next to this record was that of the Garde-Schutzen battalion, 1,000 strong, at Metz, which lost 46.1 per cent.

As striking as are these figures on the Union side they are equalled if not exceeded by those of the Confederates. It is impossible to give the figures with entire accuracy, for in making up their returns they included the losses at Harper's Ferry. South Mountain, and Antietam, aggregating 1,886 killed, 9,348 wounded, 1,377 missing, a sum total of 12,601, or according to General Lee's report, over 20 per cent. of the troops which he took into Maryland, and the greater part of which loss was sustained at Antietam.

The terrific nature of the contest sustained by them may be judged from the fact that many brigades lost one-half the men engaged, and in three at least this proportion was exceeded. Out of 42 Confederate regiments given as sustaining a loss in any one battle during the entire war of over 50 per cent., ten made this record in one day at Antietam, headed by the First Texas, of Hood's division, which lost 82.3 per cent., the highest recorded for the war.

These figures on both sides attest the bravery and obstinacy with which the opposing lines in open field, without breastworks of any kind, stood and tore each other to shreds, and your committee can say of it as was said in a report upon another field:

A field as renowned as this for the stubbornness and brilliancy of its fighting, not only in our own war, but when compared with all modern wars, has an importance to the nation as an object lesson of what is possible in American fighting, and the national value of the preservation of such lines for historical and professional study must be apparent to all reflecting minds.

The political questions which were involved in the contest ought not, under ordinary circumstances, to enter into consideration; but Antietam forms an exception, for upon the result on that field depended the greatest political stroke of modern times, the promulgation of the policy of emancipation by the President of the United States. When the summer of 1862 brought disaster to the Union cause, finally culminating in the invasion of Maryland by General Lee, Abraham Lincoln determined on the emancipation of the slaves. "I made," said Mr. Lincoln, "a solemn vow before God that if General Lee was driven back from Maryland I would crown the result by the declaration of freedom to the slaves."

General Lee was driven from Maryland, and on September 22, 1862, President Lincoln issued the proclamation.

Your committee further recommend that such bill be amended as follows: In line 8 of page 4 strike out the words "one hundred and twenty-five," and insert the word "fifty" in lieu thereof, and recommend that the bill so amended do pass.

✣ SHEPHERDSTOWN, ✣

situated on the bluffs of the southern bank of the Potomac, is like its sister town, Charles Town, an old southern, slave-holding settlement, with many marks of culture and refinement and some hereditary wealth.

It is noted as being one of the places in the valley where Gen. Hunter operated time of the war and where Lee re-crossed after the battle into Dixie at Blackford's Ford, 1 mile south of town. It is the location of one of the Confederate cemeteries, also.

BLACKFORD'S FORD,
WHERE LEE RE-CROSSED HIS ARMY INTO VIRGINIA AFTER THE BATTLE OF ANTIETAM.

THE DEVIL IN THE VALLEY.

GEN. HUNTER'S OUTRAGES AS DESCRIBED BY GEN. IMBODEN.

In a recent number of the *Atlanta Constitution*, Gen. John D. Imboden, of Virginia, describes Gen. Hunter's campaign in the Shenandoah Valley, in 1864, under the title of "The Devil in the Valley," which reads in part as follows:

After burning private property in Rockbridge county valued at over $2,000,00, and many private houses in other counties along the line of his march, he reached Shepherdstown, where, "on the 19th of July, 1864, he caused to be burned the residence of the Hon. A. R. Boteler, 'Fountain Rock.' Mrs. Boteler was also a cousin of General Hunter. This homestead was an old colonial house, endeared to the family by a thousand tender memories, and contained a splendid library, many pictures,

COL. ALEX BOTELER'S RESIDENCE,
BURNT BY GEN. HUNTER IN 1864.

and an invaluable collection of rare and precious manuscripts illustrating the early history of that part of Virginia, that Colonel Boteler had collected by years of toil. The ladies and children were at dinner when informed by the servants that a body of cavalry had turned in at the gate from the turnpike and were coming up to the house. It proved to be a small detachment of the First New York Cavalry, commanded by a Capt. William F. Martindale, who, on being met at the door by Mrs. Shepherd, coolly told her that he had come to burn the house. She asked him by what authority. He told her by that of General Hunter, and showed her his written order. "The order, I see, sir, is for you to burn the houses of Colonel Alexander Boteler and Mr. Edmund I. Lee. Now this is not Colonel Boteler's house, but is the property of my mother, Mrs. Boteler, and therefore must not be destroyed, as you have no authority to burn her house." "It's Col. Boteler's home, and that's enough for me," was Martindale's reply. She then said : "I have been obliged to remove all my personal effects here and have several thousand dollars' worth of property stored in the house and outbuildings which belongs to me and my children. Can I not be permitted to save it?" But Martindale curtly told her that he intended to "burn everything under roof upon the place." Meanwhile, some of the soldiers were plundering the house of silver spoons, forks, cups and whatever they fancied, while others piled the parlor furniture on the floors, and others poured kerosene on the piles and floors, which they then set on fire. They had brought the kerosene with them in canteens strapped to their saddles. Miss Boteler, being devoted to music, pleaded hard for her piano, as it belonged to her, having been a gift from her grandmother, but she was brutally forbidden to save it ; whereupon, although the flames were roaring in adjoining rooms, and the roof all on fire, she quietly went into the house, and seating herself for the last time before the instrument, sang her favorite, "Thy will be done." Then shutting down the lid and locking it, she calmly went out upon the lawn, where her sick sister and the frightened little children were sitting under the trees, the only shelter then left for them.

Martindale's written order from Hunter also embraced another Virginia home. He burned it too. The story is told by the gifted mistress of that household in the following letter, which was delivered to Hunter. This letter will live in history for its eloquence and sublime invective.

"*Shepherdstown, Va., July 20, 1864.*—General Hunter : Yesterday your underling, Captain Martindale, of the First New York Cavalry, executed your infamous order and burned my house. You have the satisfaction ere this of receiving from him the information that your orders were fulfilled to the letter; the dwelling and every outbuilding, seven in number, with their contents, being burned. I, therefore, a helpless woman whom you have cruelly wronged, address you, a Major-General of the United States Army, and demand why this was done! What was my offense? My husband was absent—an exile. He never had been a politician or in any way engaged in the struggle now going on, his age preventing. This fact your chief-of-staff, David Strother, could have told you. The house was built by my father—a revolutionary soldier, who served the whole seven years for your independence. There was I born; there the sacred dead repose. It was my house and my home, and there has your niece, Miss Griffith, who has tarried among us through all this horrid war up to the present moment, met with all kindness and hospitality at my hands. Was it for this that you turned me, my young daughter and little son out upon the world without a shelter? Or was it because my husband is the grandson of the revolutionary patriot and 'rebel,' Richard Henry Lee and the near kinsman of the noblest of Christian warriors, the greatest of generals, Robert E. Lee? Heaven's blessing be upon his head forever! You and your government have failed to conquer, subdue or match him, and disappointed rage and malice find vent upon the helpless and inoffensive.

"Hyena-like, you have torn my heart to pieces; for all hallowed memories clustered around that homestead; and demon-like, you have done it without even the pretext of revenge, for I never saw nor harmed you. Your office is not to lead, like a brave man and a soldier, your men to fight in the ranks of war, but your work has been to separate yourself from all danger, and with your incendiary band, steal unawares upon helpless women and children to insult and destroy. Two fair homes did you yesterday ruthlessly lay in ashes, giving not a moment's warning to the startled inmates of your wicked purpose; turning mothers and children out of doors, your very name execrated by your own men for the cruel work you gave them to do.

"In the case of Colonel A. R. Boteler, both father and mother were far away. Any heart but that of Captain Martindale (and yours) would have been touched by that little circle, comprising a widowed daughter just risen from her bed of illness, her three little fatherless babes—the oldest not five years old—and her heroic sister. I repeat, any man would have been touched at that sight. But, Captain Martindale, one might as well hope to find mercy and feeling in the heart of a wolf sent on his prey of young lambs as to search for such qualities in his bosom. You have chosen well your agent for such deeds, and doubtless will promote him!

"A Colonel of the Federal army has stated that you deprived forty of your officers of their commands because they refused to carry out your malignant mischief. All honor to their names for this, at least. They are men—they have human hearts, and they blush for such a commander.

"I ask, who that does not wish infamy and disgrace attached to him forever would serve under you! Your name will stand on history's page as the hunter of weak women and innocent children; the hunter to destroy defenseless villages and refined and beautiful homes—to torture afresh the agonized hearts of the widows; the hunter of Africa's poor sons and daughters, to lure them on to ruin and death of soul and body; the hunter with the relentless heart of a wild beast, the face of a fiend, and the form of a man. Oh, earth, behold the monster! Can I say, 'God forgive you?' No prayer can be offered for you! Were it possible for human lips to raise your name heavenward, angels would thrust the foul thing back again, and demons claim their own. The curses of thousands, the scorn of the manly and upright, and the hatred of the true and honorable, will follow you and yours through all time, and brand your name infamy! infamy!

Again, I demand why have you burned my house? Answer as you must answer before the Searcher of all hearts: why have you added this cruel, wicked deed to your many crimes?

HENRIETTA E. LEE."

"I have only recited the more prominent incidents of Hunter's brief career in the Valley of Virginia. The United States government could not stand it, his army could not stand it, as many of his prominent officers yet living tell how keenly they felt the stigma such acts—beyond their control—brought on them. Shortly after the date of Mrs. Lee's letter he was removed, to the honor of the service, and Gen. Sheridan was his successor. If the people of Chambersburg will carefully read this record of wanton destruction of private property, this 'o'er true tale' of cruel wrong inflicted on the helpless, they will understand why, when goaded to madness, remuneration was demanded at their hands by Gen. Early, and upon its refusal retaliation was inflicted on the nearest community that could be reached, and it was their misfortune to be that community. Contrast Lee in Pennsylvania in 1863 and hunter in Virginia in 1864, and judge them both as history will."

About the same time that the residences of Messrs. Boteler and Lee were burned, Gen. Hunter sent Capt. Martindale to Charles Town, with orders to burn the residence of his cousin, the Hon. Andrew Hunter, of whose generous hospitality he had frequently partaken before the war. Mr. Hunter was in Richmond, but his family were occupying the residence, the handsomest in the town, Mrs. Hunter being an invalid. Capt. Martindale exhibited his orders from Gen. Hunter and proceeded to execute them in a summary manner. Mrs. Hunter had to be carried from her home by her daughters and a servant, and Martindale turned a deaf ear to an appeal for permission to remove some prized mementos of a deceased daughter. The torch was applied in many places, and soon this beautiful residence and its valuable contents were but a heap of ashes.

FINIS.

Summer Cottages and Hotels of Harper's Ferry and Bolivar Heights.

COTTAGE OF CAPT. J. J. McCONNELL, WASHINGTON, D. C.

"CHARMADOAH," ON SHENANDOAH.
COTTAGE OF COL. H. R. MILLS, WASHINGTON, D. C.

"DUNLALLIE" ON POTOMAC, COTTAGE OF CAPT. T. M. McDUGAL, U. S. A.

"TERRACE," RESIDENCE OF MR. GEO. BREADY, HIGH STREET.

"BON AIR," ON POTOMAC, COTTAGE OF MR. CHAS. H. FISHBAUGH, WASHINGTON, D. C.

"THE OUTLOOK," BOLIVAR HEIGHTS, COTTAGE OF MRS. L. C. GOODMAN, WASHINGTON, D. C.

❧ HOTELS. ❧

HOTEL CONNER, SHENANDOAH ST., HARPER'S FERRY, S. GATRELL, PROP.

BOLIVAR HEIGHTS HOTEL, ON BOLIVAR HEIGHTS.
A. WALTER CLEVELAND AND NOAL T. WAHL, PROPS.

HILL TOP HOUSE, ON BANKS POTOMAC,
T. H. LOVETT, (COL.) PROP.

HOTEL SHENANDOAH, ON BANKS OF THE SHENANDOAH,
MISS M. L. JONES, PROPRIETRESS.

LOCKWOOD HOUSE, ON THE SHENANDOAH RIVER,
A. P. DANDRIDGE, (COL.) PROP.

McDOWELL HOUSE, ON SHENANDOAH RIVER,
BROWN E. McDOWELL, (COL.) PROP.

WAR MUSEUM OF A. SPENCER, OPPOSITE HARPER'S FERRY.

www.ingramcontent.com/pod-product-compliance
Lightning Source LLC
Chambersburg PA
CBHW020151170426
43199CB00010B/994